THE CONSTRUCTION OF CHARACTER

The Construction of Character

A Wait, Wait, Don't Query (Yet!) Book

ELENA HARTWELL

Elena Hartwell

To all the writers who persevere.

OTHER TITLES

Writing as Elena Hartwell

The Wait, Wait, Don't Query (Yet!) Series
> *The Foundation of Plot*

The Eddie Shoes Mysteries
> *One Dead, Two to Go*
> *Two Dead are Better Than One*
> *Three Strikes, You're Dead*

Writing as Elena Taylor

> *All We Buried*

CONTENTS

INTRODUCTION

> Readers connect to characters. Characters build story.

C haracters take us on an emotional ride—through how we relate to them, how they relate to each other, and the psychological journey they experience throughout the course of a story. We experience what the characters experience, regardless of genre or form. Memorable characters are key to writing memorable stories—even if a story is true. Memoir and narrative nonfiction are about people who function just as characters do in fiction.

As much as readers care about plots, no one remembers every plot point or event. Readers do, however, remember emotional responses to characters. We remember the characters we want to spend more time with; we wait impatiently for the next book in a series, or we hope a stand-alone book will generate a sequel.

While we won't remember every event in a book, we will remember how the characters made us feel.

This guide is an opportunity to analyze what makes characters tick and discover why readers connect to characters—even those they wouldn't want to know in the real world.

Whether a writer works on plot first, fleshing out characters later, or starts with complex characters, finding and refining the plot during rewrites, character and plot will be inextricable by the time a project is polished. Both elements are important, but writing and rewriting can be more productive when writers focus on one aspect at a time.

For more on plot and story structure, read *The Foundation of Plot*, another book in the Wait, Wait, Don't Query (Yet!) series.

Developing Characters

A character's objectives, backstory, and dialogue play integral roles in building the dynamic characters that readers crave.

From action/adventure to romance and from science fiction to crime fiction, readers relate to active characters driven by strong desires and concrete goals. Readers of memoir engage with an author's actions and beliefs just as much as readers of fiction engage with those of invented characters. The actions and beliefs in both genres need motivation, obstacles, and stakes.

Narrative nonfiction explores the goals and drives of real people, whether an individual, like an extreme athlete, or a group, like survivors of a natural disaster. Characters—even when they exist in the real world—propel the plot of a story through actions, thoughts, and dialogue. Memoirists mine their own histories to create the most engaging version of themselves, with a specific set of goals to focus the material.

Character objectives drive action, which drives the plot, which drives the reader through the story, creating a book—fiction or non-fiction—that's hard to put down.

That's why character objectives are so important. Reading about a character without goals is like following someone around as they aimlessly go about their day. No matter how interesting a character (or a real person) might be, following them around for no reason won't engage a reader for three hundred pages.

Characters can and should surprise readers, but that's not the same as acting out of character. Complex characters have backstories and history, but that does not mean all that information needs to be on the page. And it definitely doesn't need to appear all on page one. Deftly handling exposition and backstory can make the difference between a manuscript destined to languish forever in a desk drawer and a polished, engaging manuscript that attracts agents, editors, and readers.

Another important part of developing character is creating effective dialogue. Strong dialogue balances a sense of authenticity while also eliminating unnecessary filler words. Good dialogue is both natural and polished.

All of that and more will be discussed in *The Construction of Character*, but before we get too far, let's start with the difference between plot-driven and character-driven manuscripts, terms that are often used in the literary world.

Plot-Driven *versus* Character-Driven

Conversations in literary circles often focus on plot-driven versus character-driven stories. But what does that really mean?

Human nature has a constant need to define and categorize information. It's how we understand the world around us. We love to put items—books, movies, job titles, lifestyles—into neat boxes that help us define our experiences, explain people we meet, and guide decisions we make.

We often see the world in a series of dualities: safe/not safe, interesting/not interesting, plot-driven/character-driven.

While that duality is simplistic, for the purposes of this guide, let's define the terms this way: Plot-driven material puts action front and center. The reader is caught up in events driven by the protagonist and supporting characters. Events speed the reader through from beginning to end—think thriller and action/adventure.

Character-driven stories depend on the complexity of the characters and their relationships with each other. The unfolding of their past and its impact on their present and future is as important as their actions—think coming-of-age and romance.

What makes those definitions simplistic is that even thrillers have protagonists we root for, and romance still has action. The action in a romance may not incorporate car chases and explosions, but courtship requires action, or no one would ever get together. Think of the risks that people will take for love. Even if a romance has no sex in it, the anticipation and actions leading up to what happens after "the end" will engage readers.

Some books and some genres lend themselves toward more introspection by the characters and their dependence on relationships with other characters than on the actions the characters take. But even then, characters still take actions.

By the time we finish this guidebook, it will be clear that a polished manuscript is more than just plot-driven or character-driven, but understanding that distinction is enough to get us started. Those terms provide a shorthand for discussing particular manuscripts and conventions in a genre. Just keep in mind that character-driven stories need action, and plot-driven stories need characters.

Creative Child and Critical Eye

One concept I find useful when writing and rewriting is the difference between the creative child and the critical eye. As discussed in *The Foundation of Plot*, the creative child comes into play when a writer lets their imagination loose. The creative child does not judge or censor but rather explores a story through words on the page.

The critical eye is the adult in the writing process, editing and shaping the rough clay which the child hands over when the work gets hard. It's the critical eye that cuts out great material if it doesn't serve the manuscript. It's the critical eye pushing the writer to hit those writing goals, even when those goals feel like work.

To apply those two concepts to building characters, the creative child can be very useful for imagining the biggest obstacles and the wildest objectives. The creative child can also dream up dialogue, free from the anxiety of whether it's "good enough." The critical eye, on the other hand, can take big obstacles the creative child throws at the character and dig into the emotional state of the character with more rigor, understanding exactly how those obstacles play out, with more nuance and authenticity than a child can.

Both the creative child and the critical eye are imperative for writers. We need the freedom to create, unfettered by anxiety, but we also need to analyze our own work with the clinical detachment of an outside eye.

This guidebook includes exercises at the end of each chapter to apply to a work in progress or a new project. Let's get started with one designed to identify which side has more control in our writing: the creative child or the critical eye. It can be useful to know which side comes easier and which side needs more attention so we can shift between them easily and equally. We may also discover we need to buckle down and use the critical eye to edit our existing material or engage the creative child to let our imaginations loose, let go of self-censorship, and produce those early draft pages.

Exercise 1: Creative Child or Critical Eye

Write about the main character in a current work in progress. If starting a brand-new project, use this exercise to begin developing a main character.

Step One: Respond to each prompt. Set an alarm for three to five minutes for each one. Keep writing. Don't censor; just let the words flow.

(Name of main character) loves ...

(Name of main character) fears ...

(Name of main character) would describe themselves like this:

Characters closest to (name of main character) would describe them as ...

Step Two: Go back through the material from Step One and rewrite. Fix the language and adjust the content to make it clearer and better constructed, but save the original draft for comparison.

Step Three: Reflect on all the generated material. What new information became available about the character in both drafts? This information will be useful in future exercises and during rewrites.

Which part of the exercise came more naturally?

If the freewrite was easier, the creative child may be closer to the surface. If the rewriting came easier, the critical eye may be a more comfortable fit. If the two were equal, that could show balance. There's no right or wrong answer to this. It's solely information about approaching writing and getting focused.

Stuck? Let the creative child loose. Lots of unfocused material? Bring in the critical eye.

Now that we have a basic context for this guidebook and content to use for future exercises, let's look closer at some character basics.

| 1 |

A Few Basics

> Authenticity in writing comes from being
> yourself, not from writing what you know.

Characters reflect the world we live in, even in universes that spring solely from a writer's imagination. When characters exist in a purely imaginary world, they still face challenges that echo our own, which is part of why we read those genres—they allow us to view human issues against a fun and fantastical backdrop.

Characters are most effective when they are complicated and faced with challenges. That means there is room for a variety of characters, with different ages, ethnicities, socioeconomic statuses, religions, and political beliefs. Most importantly, that diversity can be illustrated with a complexity of emotions and motivations, keeping our characters from turning into cardboard cutouts.

Every writer is capable of creating unique and dynamic characters. If static characters are something a writer struggles with, it's likely a craft problem, not a talent problem. By learning the craft of creating complex characters, any writer can build engaging characters and a successful manuscript.

When creating authentic characters, we bring our own understanding of the human condition to our work, reflecting our individual backgrounds, philosophies, and psychologies. No writer will ever build the same character as another writer, even if starting from the same character description, because we each have a unique understanding of the world.

This unique understanding is part of what defines an author's voice. Authenticity comes from our understanding of the world, not from mimicking someone else's beliefs or style.

Building complexity comes from applying that understanding to our characters. When a writer combines research, observations of others, and thoughtfulness about how people think, feel, and react, complex characters are guaranteed.

The old adage "write what you know" can become "write what you understand."

We might balk at certain issues when constructing characters, which can interfere with creating complexity. For example, it can be a challenge to build characters we don't like or who express beliefs that are different from our own without turning those characters into buffoons. But without diverse characters with differing opinions and values, manuscripts can fall flat and fail to reflect the world in an authentic way. If every character thinks the same, there's no conflict.

Embrace every aspect of humanity, from killers who love dogs to loving mothers who don't protect their children to cautious people who act out in irresponsible ways.

This leads to two of the challenges to building solid characters: creating unlikeable characters and putting characters we love in danger. Both challenges can be useful tools in writing an engaging manuscript.

Likeable versus Unlikeable

It's tempting to fill our manuscripts with characters we like. After all, we spend months if not years with these individuals, and it can feel safer and easier psychologically if we like them.

But that doesn't always translate well for readers.

Readers love to have characters to hate. Further, protagonists can't get along with everyone. Part of creating conflict is to have characters in opposition to our main character. That doesn't mean they have to fight constantly, but they will have conflicting agendas.

We can create conflict through good characters who want different things, but unlikeable characters can also add a lot of spice.

Some of the most memorable characters of all time have been "bad guys." Nurse Ratched, Cruella de Vil, Lord Voldemort—evil characters make their mark and keep readers engaged, sometimes even more than the "good guys."

Creating an unlikeable protagonist can turn a tepid work into a compelling page-turner. Readers love to see an unlikeable protagonist get what's coming to them; this makes the book impossible to put down until the character either changes or suffers what they deserve.

A criticism that sometimes gets leveled at books is, "I didn't like the main character." That can be a legitimate assessment. Asking readers to follow someone for three hundred pages when they don't like that character is a big ask. But readers can also confuse characters who are not engaging with characters they don't like.

Having a character with clear goals is more important than likeability. A character can be unlikeable, and readers will still connect if that character has clear goals, big obstacles, and high stakes. That makes a character engaging far more than likeability.

We will delve into objectives, obstacles, and stakes in greater detail in Chapter Four, but for now, consider which character is more compelling solely from the description:

Character A: A single mom whose daughter vanishes.

Character B: A single mom who, when her daughter vanishes, will do everything necessary to track her down and bring her home.

Most of us will be drawn to Character B. It's her story that we want to follow.

The fact that Character A's daughter vanishes may pique our curiosity, but without the goal of tracking her daughter down, there's nothing to pull us in and make us curious to learn more. For all we know, the manuscript is about grieving the missing daughter, without any compelling action included at all.

With no information to help us determine if we would like one of these characters more than the other, we are already drawn toward Character B because she has a clear objective. This simple example indicates our willingness to follow characters with objectives over characters without objectives, regardless of likeability.

A better way to think about characters may be their relatability, not their likeability.

Relatable Characters

Creating universal characters is a common goal for writers. But one common error that writers make is to assume that generalities make a character more relatable and universal when in fact, the opposite is true.

The more specific we make our characters' goals and obstacles, the more readers will relate to them—not because the character's goals are identical to those of the reader, but because the goals can be understood by the reader. We relate to characters with parallel goals, not identical ones.

Readers relate to a character's objectives not because they want the same thing, but because they understand the importance of a character's goal through understanding the importance of their own hopes and dreams.

For example, a reader does not need to have children to understand that a child's well-being is important to a parent. Readers who don't have children still have nieces, nephews, cousins, and friends. For some of us, our love for our pets can be translated into what it means to care for a child.

What resonates for a reader is concern for another person, especially a vulnerable person. It doesn't matter that the reader is not a single mother worried about her teenage daughter.

Consider a reader who cares for an aging parent and wants to provide the best for them. That could involve a difficult choice: working extra hours to pay for the best care facility or working fewer hours in order to spend more time with their parent. That reader would relate to a mother wanting to send her daughter to the best private school—not because their situations are identical, but because they are similar. That's what makes it understandable for the reader.

A reader who struggles over whether to pay a utility bill or pay for medication would understand as well, even without another person dependent on them. Financial struggles are universal, regardless of how those issues manifest.

Putting Characters in Danger

It can be hard to put much-loved characters in danger. They are part of us and reflective of us, so we want to protect them.

But that's not what readers want.

Readers want to see characters suffer and struggle and persevere. Regardless of genre, readers need characters to overcome obstacles; otherwise, there's no tension in the plot.

Tension creates the drive to see what happens next. Page-turners are built out of manuscripts with tension. Tension is created, in large part, by the conflict among a character's actions, obstacles, and stakes.

Take Character B (let's call her Patricia) and add some danger to her situation using the financial scenario above. Patricia is a single mom, working hard to support her daughter, Kelly. She works endless hours because she wants to enroll her daughter in a better school. Kelly has fallen in with a bad crowd. Patricia knows she needs to spend more time with her daughter, but she can't make ends meet if she doesn't work as many hours as she can. This puts conflict into the story—internal conflict. (We'll talk more about conflict in Chapter Six.)

Kelly gets into more and more trouble, leaving Patricia unsure what will help her daughter most: cut back her work hours and spend more time with Kelly, or work more hours and transfer Kelly to an expensive private school.

It may feel that the danger here is to Kelly, not Patricia. But danger can be physical, emotional, or psychological. In this example, Patricia's emotional well-being is impacted by her concern for her daughter's future. Emotional danger is actual danger. Plus, a child's well-being and future success are very real concerns for any good parent.

Patricia has become a more empathetic character because of this tension, even though we know nothing else about her. We haven't met her; we've only expanded her description, so whether she's likeable or not remains to be seen, but we have created a more relatable character because we see her conflict about how to best help her child.

Adding to the conflict, both solutions to help her daughter are "good" ones. It's easy to choose between a good and a bad decision. It's harder, and creates more empathy, to choose between two good choices (or two bad choices). A better school or more quality time are both good, but Patricia can only choose one.

As we move forward with creating characters, keep these three takeaways in mind:

- Creating a likeable character is less important than creating a character with clear goals.
- Relatability built through specific choices makes characters feel universal. A character and a reader need not experience the identical event or situation.
- Putting a character in danger—emotional, psychological, or physical—increases a reader's empathy toward a character, which makes the character more important to the reader.

Exercise 2: Character Relatability

Let's identify what makes a character relatable. This will stem, in large part, from the character's super-objective, which we cover in greater detail in Chapter Four. To get started defining a super-objective, let's take a big picture look at the character, whether that character has taken shape in a work in progress or is brand new.

The following exercise can be applied to any character; however, starting with the protagonist will likely be the most constructive, especially if this is a new project.

Step One: What does the character want at the beginning of the manuscript? If the beginning has already been drafted, use the critical eye and assess if the character has a clear goal. If so, define that goal. If not, engage the creative child in a freewrite and determine what the goal might be.

Struggling with a brand-new project and don't yet have a goal for an imagined protagonist? Consider what that character wants at the beginning of the story. Use the creative child to imagine the biggest goal possible. If that doesn't work, bring in the critical eye to force a goal, but don't worry about whether or not it's "right."

Step Two: If you've written a beginning, determine how to rewrite it to make the goal clearer. If the beginning is not yet written, determine what needs to happen in a scene to show readers the character's primary goal. Don't write or rewrite the material yet; just mull the possibilities.

Write a few paragraphs defining how to either make that goal clearer in the beginning or how an opening scene might show what the character wants. Work to determine how to approach the writing or rewriting to clarify the goal. Sit with what those scenes need to accomplish. Don't rush.

Part of writing and rewriting is to have a clear objective before sitting down to the computer or notebook. Writer's block does not exist; what we call writer's block is just an unprepared writer sitting down to work without a clear goal. By preparing ahead of time and having writing goals, including the broad strokes of a scene, the writing time will be more productive.

It's better to have a goal that is later changed or built upon than to have no sense of what a character wants. It's much easier to generate scenes if we know what a character's ultimate goals are, because every action moves toward achieving that goal.

Keep the information from this exercise handy; we'll come back to it later.

| 2 |

Viewpoint Character versus Protagonist

> Everyone has a story to tell, but it's not always their own.

Two important facets of primary characters should thread through a manuscript: the character whose story we follow (protagonist or main character) and the character or characters through whose eyes we view events (viewpoint character).

The protagonist is the main character. They are the character (or person, in memoir/narrative nonfiction) who readers follow through the story. They are the character whose actions drive the plot, reach the climax, and provide closure at the end. They are usually the character that readers care about the most.

A story can have more than one protagonist, whether it's in fiction, with more than one main character serving as a protagonist, or in narrative nonfiction, when a group (such as survivors of a natural disaster) collectively serves as the protagonist. For characters to be true protagonists, however, and not just major characters, they must be equal in importance. Sometimes writers confuse important characters with the protagonist. Gandalf is an important character in *The Hobbit*, but Bilbo is the protagonist.

The viewpoint character is the character through whose eyes readers experience events.

Sherlock Holmes is the protagonist. Watson is the viewpoint character.

It's easy to confuse the viewpoint character with the main character or protagonist. Part of what complicates the distinction is that sometimes the viewpoint character is the protagonist, and sometimes it's not.

Before we work on making characters complex and unique, let's go over a few key definitions so we have a common vocabulary and understand how each of these facets of character function.

These concepts also define some of the most important choices a writer can make, as they impact everything that's available to the author and the reader in terms of the presentation of the story.

Viewpoint Character

The viewpoint character is the character through whose eyes a reader experiences a scene. Further, the point of view the author writes in—first person, second person, or third person (limited or omniscient) —determines what information can be accessed by the reader.

For example, if the viewpoint character is a single person, let's say a private eye, and that character's point of view is first person, then only the information immediately in front of that private eye, experienced by that private eye, or known by that private eye can be provided for the reader using "I" as the voice of the character.

I walked into the room. It was too dark to see if anyone hid behind the desk.

The reader can't know if someone hides behind the desk because the private eye doesn't know if anyone hides behind the desk.

We'll go deeper into point of view in Chapter Three, but first, it will help to understand how viewpoint character and protagonist can differ.

Protagonist

Readers follow the protagonist for the majority if not all of the scenes. The protagonist is the individual with the biggest objectives, obstacles, and stakes. Readers root for the protagonist and track their story from beginning to end. This character often starts and ends the manuscript, though occasionally they don't appear in a prologue or first chapter. If the protagonist doesn't arrive by the second chapter, that may be a structural problem, or the writer chose the wrong character as the protagonist.

If another character in a work in progress takes up more space and importance than the current protagonist, that other character may be the actual protagonist, and the writer has misidentified who the manuscript is about. That can happen when working through early drafts, and it only matters if the writer doesn't identify the protagonist before finalizing a polished draft and starting to query. My hope is that by the end of this guidebook, the protagonist, viewpoint character, and point of view will be crystal clear.

Sometimes writers choose to have another character tell the story of the protagonist. In that situation, the viewpoint character and protagonist can be confusing.

Consider this: The protagonist is Patricia's daughter Kelly, but the viewpoint character is Patricia, and Patricia's point of view is in first person. In other words, Kelly is the main character, but the character who relays the events to the reader is Patricia, and she does so using words like I, we, and me.

Let's see what that might look like.

My daughter Kelly experienced an extraordinary event. She's too shy to tell you about it, but I'm not.

That opening line shows the reader that the manuscript is about Kelly; she is the protagonist. It's her experiences that we are going to learn about and care about the most. But the viewpoint character is Patricia, and the story will be in first person point of view. This only works, however, in past tense, with Patricia able to tell the story as shared with her by Kelly. Patricia can't tell us anything about Kelly that Kelly has not shared with her, nor can she tell Kelly's story in present tense, unless she's with her.

Another option is for Patricia to be both the viewpoint character and the protagonist. We might start out like this:

I arrived home that day expecting my daughter Kelly to be in her room, pretending to do her homework while clicking through Instagram reels and DMing with her friends.

This sentence shows readers that they will follow Patricia's story, and, while her daughter will be an important character, Patricia is both the protagonist and the viewpoint character. In this example, the story is told in first person point of view.

Each point of view has pros and cons, which we'll discuss in greater detail in Chapter Three. But before we do that, let's take a quick look at multiple protagonists.

Multiple Protagonists versus Multiple Viewpoint Characters

Another convention that can confuse writers is the difference between multiple viewpoint characters and multiple protagonists.

This brings us back to the issue of who a manuscript is about, a fundamental but sometimes tricky decision to make.

Using multiple viewpoint characters is a common convention in several different genres. Consider all the thrillers with most chapters in the viewpoint of the hero, interspersed with chapters in the viewpoint of the villain. Romance novels might include chapters from the viewpoints of both characters in a relationship. A science fiction novel could include chapters from the viewpoints of different members of a deep space exploration crew.

But that does not mean that each of these characters is a protagonist. They are only protagonists if they equally drive events, participate in forcing the climax, provide resolutions, and if readers are equally invested in their character and story arcs.

If there is more than one primary character of equal importance, that is an example of multiple protagonists.

If the characters are equal in importance, share equal time on the page, and are equal in terms of who readers root for—each with strong objectives, obstacles, and stakes—they could be equal protagonists. For example, *One Two Three* by Laurie Frankel has three equal protagonists, which she even identifies in the title. Each sister, identified by their birth order as One, Two, and Three, have equal time on the page, and readers follow each of their stories throughout the entire manuscript. Different chapters are presented in each sister's viewpoint, making them viewpoint characters and protagonists.

That's different than a story with one protagonist who remains the main character regardless of the inclusion of other viewpoint characters.

Several examples exist of multiple viewpoint characters with a single protagonist. Consider this scenario: A detective races around finding clues, chasing the killer, and solving the crime. But the author includes a few chapters through the eyes of the killer or a victim. That does not change the fact that the detective is the protagonist. The detective remains the primary character, even if there is a chapter with the killer as the viewpoint character.

If, however, the killer and the detective share an equal number of chapters, are equal in importance, and have equally big objectives, obstacles, and stakes, that would be an example of multiple protagonists. Protagonists don't have to be "good guys." They are just the most important character in the story.

Viewpoint Character and Protagonist: Why the Distinction Matters

It's important to know who the viewpoint character is because that is the character who creates the parameters for what information can be shown or told to readers and how. Readers can only access information available to the viewpoint character, based on the point of view the author chooses (first, second, or third person).

We will go deeper into point of view in the next chapter. What's important to understand now is that the protagonist drives the bulk of the action; they are the most important character, with the biggest role and the most scenes. The viewpoint character shows the events to the reader.

Which character tells a story and whose story they tell are two of the most important decisions a writer can make. Combined with point of view (first, second, or third person), those decisions determine the rules the manuscript will follow, including what readers can and cannot be shown.

During the drafting process, knowing who drives events can help determine which events make it onto the page. It can also determine how those events build on each other to create the plot. To learn more about that part of the process, read *The Foundation of Plot*, another book in the Wait, Wait, Don't Query (Yet!) series.

Major Players are Still Secondary Characters

The main character, whether they are the viewpoint character or not, will drive the bulk of the action. But they may not be the only major player.

Other characters can come close to taking center stage but remain secondary; therefore, they are not protagonists. When a writer creates other major characters, especially when they share a lot of page time and drive a lot of the action, they can feel like protagonists. But as mentioned earlier, it's vital to discern between a major character and a protagonist.

Consider the sidekick who appears in almost every scene. Or the viewpoint character who tells the story, as Dr. Watson does for Sherlock Holmes. It might feel like Dr. Watson is the protagonist, but he's not; the actions of Sherlock Holmes drive the story.

It's easy to think there is more than one protagonist if another character also drives the action and impacts the plot throughout the manuscript, but that isn't necessarily the case—the story may not require two protagonists. We can identify a major character as secondary when they are not quite as important to the story as the protagonist. They might lead a subplot, but even that does not make them a protagonist.

In my private eye series, the Eddie Shoes mysteries, I write in first person point of view, with Eddie Shoes as the private eye. She teams up with her mother Chava to solve homicides. Chava plays a central role in every book, but it's not her story—it's Eddie's. That makes Chava a major player but not a protagonist.

One important aspect of this concept is that we don't need all the major players as viewpoint characters, even if they are integral to the plot. Chava is never a viewpoint character; she's only seen through Eddie's eyes. It's okay to always see secondary characters from another character's viewpoint. It's also important to understand that other major characters can't be the ones to take center stage at the climax. Let the protagonist have their moment to shine, even if they reach the climax with help from other characters.

Minor Characters

Just as major characters can play important roles, minor characters can make a manuscript pop. In book three of the Eddie Shoes books, Jake the firefighter plays an important role even though he doesn't appear in many scenes. He provides a possible romantic partner for Eddie, forcing her to decide what to do about a relationship she has previously failed to pursue. Readers love to connect to everyone who appears on the page, and the minor characters can be as complex as any other character, no matter the size of their role.

To make even the most minor of characters stand out, consider physical appearance and dialogue. By providing readers with something specific about physical appearance, even the most minor of characters can become memorable.

Consider the following exchange.

Patricia arrived at the bus station. She crossed to the ticket window and tapped on the glass.

"Can I help you?" the clerk asked.

"Were you working here yesterday afternoon?"

"Yes."

"Great. Do you recognize this girl?" Patricia held up her cell phone with a recent photo of Kelly.

"She doesn't look familiar."

"She might have bought a ticket yesterday."

"No. Sorry."

This exchange does provide the information we need for the scene, but the clerk is unremarkable, adding nothing to the flavor of the material.

Consider this instead:

Patricia arrived at the bus station. Crossing to the ticket window, she spied an elderly woman behind the counter, her gray hair in a tight bun.

"Help you?" Her voice boomed from the window. Patricia noticed hearing aids in the woman's ears.

"Were you working here yesterday afternoon?"

"Every weekday, rain or shine, God willing."

"Great. Do you recognize this girl?" Patricia held up her cell phone with a recent photo of Kelly.

"Such a pretty young thing. She's got your eyes."

"She might have bought a ticket yesterday."

The woman took the phone in one veined hand. She pulled up the reading glasses that hung around her neck on a rhinestone keeper. She stared long and hard, but finally clucked her tongue and handed the phone back.

"I'm so sorry, but I've never seen her. I would have remembered a young girl like that."

This exchange fleshes out the nameless clerk. Readers will remember her. Readers will also have an emotional reaction to her; whether it's good or bad depends on the reader's own experiences, but regardless, this character has her own voice.

No matter how interesting and engaging another major or minor character is, however, that doesn't mean they should have chapters or scenes as viewpoint characters. Writers need a good reason for a viewpoint character to share the stage with another viewpoint character. If we are going to spend time in more than one character's head, it has to be worth pulling the reader away from a character they are already engaged with, especially at the beginning.

Now that we have a clearer understanding of the importance of identifying the protagonist and viewpoint character, let's do an exercise to help determine the strongest choice for a work in progress or for a brand-new project started through the earlier exercises in this book.

Exercise 3: Viewpoint Character and Protagonist

Sometimes identifying the protagonist is easy. If it's a mystery about someone solving a homicide, the detective—professional or amateur— is usually the main character. But in other scenarios, identifying the main character can be trickier. For example, three characters work together to save their community from an evil warlord in a sci-fi novel. Which one is the protagonist? How about a historical novel about a family overcoming a tragedy, with each family member performing an important role?

In both of those examples, one character will likely still take center stage. For example, in the original *Star Wars*, Luke Skywalker, Princess Leia, and Han Solo all play integral roles, but Luke is the main character, while Leia and Han Solo are important major characters.

In early drafts, it can be hard to identify which character is the actual protagonist or if a work truly has more than one.

For this exercise, let's examine how clear the protagonist and viewpoint characters are for a work in progress, or keep building characters from the first two exercises.

Step One: For a work in progress or a new work, read the material you have so far, whether it's an entire draft or only the material from the first two exercises. Is it easy to identify the protagonist?

If so, great. Write this down: The protagonist is ... (fill in the blank). I know this because ... (fill in the blank).

If the main character isn't clear, put five minutes on a timer and see what the creative child comes up with, without censorship. To engage the creative child, use the following prompt and do a freewrite:

Writing Prompt: The character with the most important story is ...

If that still doesn't identify a single protagonist, consider that there may be more than one protagonist. It's okay to work on a draft with more than one protagonist, as the true protagonist may become clear during the drafting process. Or embrace the challenge of creating multiple characters of equal value to readers. Come back and do this exercise again after the draft begins to take shape.

Step Two: Identify who tells the story of the protagonist. Does the protagonist tell their own story? Does another character or an outside narrator tell the story? If the protagonist isn't clear, the viewpoint character may be the protagonist. Go ahead and do this part of the exercise even if the first part is still in flux.

Writing Prompt: The viewpoint character is ... (fill in the blank). I know this because ... (fill in the blank).

If it's the same character as the protagonist, great. That's often the easiest path. If it's not, don't worry—by the end of this guidebook, the path forward should be clear, whether the manuscript will have one protagonist as viewpoint character, one viewpoint character and another character as protagonist, or multiple viewpoint characters, but only one protagonist. All of those scenarios, and more, are viable; the characters' roles just need to be understood and used appropriately.

| 3 |

Point of View

Point of view is about more than just I, you, he, or she.
It's also about the information available to the reader and the
reader's closeness to the viewpoint character.

Once the viewpoint character (or characters) has been identified, the writer can use "I," "you," or "he/she/they." The I, you, and he/she/they indicate different points of view. We call those first, second, and third person point of view. Third person can be limited, limited (close), multiple, or omniscient.

Authors often have a favorite point of view used consistently across each book they write. Other authors might use different points of view for different books. In my Eddie Shoes mysteries, I use first person point of view, while my standalone police procedural, *All We Buried*, uses third person (limited) point of view.

One Dead, Two to Go, the first book in the Eddie Shoes series, starts out like this: "Call me Eddie Shoes." This is written in first person point of view, using "I/me" for the character narrating the story. Eddie is also the sole viewpoint character, and every scene in the book comes through her perspective.

All We Buried starts this way: "Sheriff Bet Rivers leaned back in her chair and gazed out the office window at the shifting light on Lake

Collier." This is written in third person, using "she/her." Bet Rivers is the viewpoint character, with every scene in the book highlighting her perspective. This is an example of third person limited point of view, which will be discussed in greater detail later in this chapter.

There is no right or wrong choice for point of view, only what fits best for any given project.

Lee Child, in writing his Jack Reacher books, uses first person point of view for six of his novels, including the first book, *Killing Floor*. Child wrote the other books in the series, twenty-six at the time I wrote this, in third person limited point of view.

Every option is open to every writer, regardless of what they have done in the past.

To better understand how point of view functions in a story, let's step through the different points of view.

First Person

First person point of view is the "I" point of view. Memoirists write almost entirely in first person point of view since it's their life story told from their own perspective. But fiction writers can use first person as well. It's quite common, with more than fifty percent of fiction and 99.99 percent of memoir written in first person point of view.

This point of view has many benefits. Writing in first person is intimate; it puts the reader directly inside the character's head—a character who is most likely also the protagonist. As an example of first person point of view, let's start a scene with the character we have been developing over the course of this book, Patricia, mom to a teenage girl, Kelly.

I walked into the kitchen expecting to find Kelly at the table doing her homework. Instead, I found a few dirty dishes in the sink and the cat asleep in the window seat. The dishes proved that Kelly had been there, but the empty room sent a shiver down my spine. The house sat too quiet.

Notice that readers are only able to access what Patricia experiences, but it also feels like we are right beside her, seeing and feeling what she's seeing and feeling. She can see the dirty dishes; she knows what they signal and can share with readers that her daughter did come home from school. Readers do not have access to where Kelly is now because Patricia doesn't have that information.

First person point of view works great for situations where the author doesn't want or need to provide information about multiple characters outside what the viewpoint character can experience. Because Patricia doesn't know where Kelly is, we can't show readers where Kelly is, but that's okay because part of the tension in the story stems from neither Patricia nor the reader knowing the teenager's whereabouts.

Patricia is also the protagonist, so not having access to information about Kelly works fine. If Kelly was the protagonist, and never the viewpoint character, we would have an issue because we can't access her through Patricia unless Patricia has information about Kelly from either Kelly herself or someone in direct contact with her.

Writing in past tense, we could fill in some of the blanks about where Kelly was and what she experienced, but only as much as Patricia learns after the fact from either Kelly or people Kelly interacted with. Patricia can't know that information until Kelly returns or someone who knows the situation enters the story.

But with Patricia as both the viewpoint character and the protagonist, we can build tension because we don't know any more than Patricia does. Her tension becomes our tension.

If we wanted to let readers know where Kelly is and what she's doing, first person point of view wouldn't work very well unless we interspersed Patricia's chapters with chapters from another viewpoint character, such as Kelly or another character interacting with Kelly or otherwise aware of her actions, such as a stalker. Patricia would still be the protagonist, but we could include chapters with Kelly or someone else as a viewpoint character, but not a protagonist. Readers could then have information that Patricia doesn't have, even though Patricia is the main character. Our tension would then come from wondering if, when, and how Patricia will discover that information.

We could also have Kelly and Patricia equal in terms of page time and importance. That would turn this manuscript into a multiple protagonist project. At that point, we would decide whether both characters are written in first, second, or third person point of view, and they would not have to use the same point of view. Some books alternate point of view, such as having Kelly's chapters or sections in third person limited and Patricia's in first person.

Readers love the internal thoughts available through first person point of view. It allows us to be close to the character in a way that even third person limited point of view can't do. With first person point of view, we hear the character's internal voice, which is not the case with third person.

First person point of view does restrict what information we can provide readers because everything filters through the "I" point of view. But we can also build a rapport between readers and our first-person viewpoint character in a way that other point of views might not.

Second Person

Second person point of view is rarely used. It's primarily found in literary fiction and poetry. It can work to great effect, but it can also grate on a reader's nerves as it creates an odd bridge between the character and the reader, almost as if the reader becomes a character. It can also be written with both an unidentified "you" and an identified "you." This means that we can write directly to readers as "you" or create a specific character whom we address as "you."

If we took the same scene that we just wrote in first person and rewrote it in second person point of view with a an unidentified "you" (making the reader "you"), it might look like this:

You walked into the kitchen expecting to find Kelly at the table doing her homework. Instead, you found a few dirty dishes in the sink and the cat asleep in the window seat. The dishes proved Kelly had been home, but the empty room sent a shiver down your spine. The house sat too quiet to have a teenager inside its walls.

The "you" here places the reader into the story in a very different way than using "I." With first person point of view, the reader is the fly on the wall. With second person point of view, the reader enters the story as if they are Patricia or another character.

If we wanted to rewrite with "you" as another identified character in the story, we might write this as if we are speaking to Kelly herself:

You should have been at the table, doing your homework. Instead, there were only a few dirty dishes in the sink and the cat asleep in the window seat. The dishes proved that you had been home after school, but the empty room screamed the fact you weren't there now.

Two successful books written in second person point of view are *Bright Lights, Big City* by Jay McInerney and *Winter Journal* by Paul Auster. *Winter Journal* is a memoir, so writing it in second person is doubly unusual (and why, at the start of the chapter, I identified memoir as being written in first person point of view 99.99 percent of the time). Auster is a literary author, so his voice consists of exquisite language which adds to the unusual tone of the work. *Bright Lights, Big City* is both humorous and literary, which makes second person point of view effective, and it's also part of the coming of age and satire genres, which have more flexibility compared to the expectations in other genres.

It would be a challenge, though not impossible, to make second person point of view work well for a thriller or a fantasy novel. Certain categories of books lend themselves more readily to this less common point of view, and genre fiction authors may want to steer clear of using it if the goal is a commercial, more easily marketed novel—especially if those novels are not crossovers into literary fiction and the writer is a debut author.

There is nothing wrong with writing in second person, but anything that pushes a novel into a more limited readership can also make it less attractive to agents and editors and harder to sell.

Authors make choices based on both art and business. It's fine for a writer to write the book they want to write, but limiting readership will limit marketability and potentially limit the book to self-publishing or a small publisher. That's an author's choice to make, but one to be made with a clear understanding of the restrictions it creates.

Third Person Limited

Third person limited point of view uses he, she, or they (where "they" indicates a group, a nonbinary character, or a character for whom gender is unknown.) This point of view focuses on one character, which is different from third person omniscient point of view, which follows multiple characters from a distance. The distance is created because the narrator is outside each character. They may have access to information in the character's mind, but they are never the character themselves.

Let's look at the previous short scene with Patricia as our viewpoint character and third person limited as our point of view.

Patricia walked into the kitchen expecting to find Kelly at the table doing her homework. Instead, she found only a few dirty dishes in the sink and the cat asleep in the window seat. The dishes proved Kelly had been home, but the empty room sent a shiver down Patricia's spine. The house sat too quiet.

Notice the use of Patricia's name to introduce the scene, clarifying with the first sentence that we are using third person point of view. With first person, the story started with I, as Patricia wouldn't think of herself by her given name. (When writing in first person, we must find other ways to introduce our character's name, such as another character saying it in a line of dialogue.)

The use of "they" can help clarify whether a person's gender is unknown or if they are nonbinary, but be aware that it can create confusion for the reader if it's unclear just who "they" refers to: a person or a group.

Consider the following if Patricia were nonbinary.

They walked into the kitchen expecting to find Kelly at the table doing her homework. Instead, they found a few dirty dishes in the sink and the cat asleep in the window seat. The dishes proved Kelly had been home, but the empty room sent a shiver down their spine. The house sat too quiet to house a teenager.

"They" is clear if we set up at the beginning of the novel that Patricia is nonbinary and uses "they" as a pronoun, but in another context, it could be unclear who "they" refers to. Consider the following:

Patricia found Kelly at the park. They got into the car and drove home.

In this instance, we might mean that both parent and child got into the car. But it could also mean that Patricia found Kelly and, satisfied that their daughter was all right, left her there and went home. To clarify, this might need to be written this way: *Patricia found Kelly at the park. Together, they got in the car and drove home.* Or: *Patricia found Kelly at the park. Trusting their daughter to come home before curfew, they went home alone.*

This does not mean that a writer can't use "they," but it will require extra attention for clarity when used as a singular pronoun.

The term "limited" in third person limited point of view means that only what the viewpoint character experiences can be translated to the reader. There is a little more leeway with regard to descriptions, however, than there is with first person point of view because there is a slight distance between the reader and the third person limited narrator, even though it's minor.

To describe that further, consider this in first person point of view:

I walked up the steps of the front porch, expecting the front door to be unlocked. Kelly never remembered to lock the door behind her. The knob held fast; the house was locked up tight. Concerned, I pulled the keys out of my purse and jiggled the sticky lock. Pushing the door open, I called out Kelly's name as I entered.

The specifics are what Patricia would be conscious of as she's doing these actions. It makes sense to the reader that she would be aware of all those details. But if we use third person, we can expand on the details.

Patricia walked up the steps. The porch creaked, as it had for the last two decades on the old Craftsman-style house. Reaching out, she expected to find the door unlocked. Kelly never remembered to lock the door. The brass knob held fast, locked up tight. A shiver of fear bolted through Patricia as she dug in her hobo bag for her keys. The lock stuck because it was a touch out of alignment, but with an expert jiggle, she popped open the door. Calling out as she entered, Patricia could sense her daughter wasn't home.

Both paragraphs work. They both show Patricia coming home and realizing her daughter isn't there. In the first-person example, it feels like we are zeroed in on Patricia's emotions and reactions. In the third person limited example, we can add details about the house that Patricia wouldn't think about as she's doing the actions of coming home, but these are details she would know; therefore, they can be included.

Different points of view can cause limitations depending on a character's knowledge and experience.

Consider this situation. Patricia's car breaks down. She's not a mechanic. If we write that in first person point of view, we can't diagnose the car trouble:

The car made a chunka-chunka-chunka sound before coasting listlessly to the side of the road. I wanted to cry.

Let's try third person limited point of view: *The water pump finally gave up trying to keep the old Volvo cool, leaving the last of its water on the pavement as the engine seized. Patricia wanted to cry.*

It's up to the writer to determine how to show the event. But with first person point of view, we experience the car breaking down as Patricia experiences it, and she knows nothing about cars. In the second example, we can add the details because we are distanced from the character and can expand on what she might know. Patricia would certainly learn about the water pump later when she has the car towed the car to a garage, and as this is written in past tense, she can "know" that in this scenario.

Like first person point of view, third person limited keeps us tied to only what the viewpoint character experiences. While we do have access to more detail, as with the examples of the description of the house and car, we can't add a paragraph about what Kelly is doing or anything too far outside of Patricia's frame of reference. We do have room for details outside of Patricia, but we have to be careful about including information she can't access. We can get away with showing that the water pump gave up because conceivably, Patricia either knows it was failing and hadn't fixed it, or as mentioned above, with past tense, she knows what failed on her car because of what she learned after having the car repaired. We can also include more information outside of her experiences if we write with more distance between the narrator and the viewpoint character. That distance between the narrator to the viewpoint character can help writers determine how much can be included that Patricia wouldn't know. We will go into closeness later in this chapter.

Choosing point of view is up to the writer. Just keep in mind that choice determines what's available to show or tell the reader.

Third Person Limited (Close)

Third person limited (close) point of view is slightly more intimate than third person limited. Think of it as combining aspects of first person with aspects of third. With third person limited (close), the writer removes anything that puts the reader at a distance from the character, even though that character's point of view remains in third person. Here is an example of what that might look like.

Third person limited: *Patricia glanced around the kitchen. There was no sign of Kelly's book bag or cell phone. Her sneakers were not in the hallway. Kelly always left her sneakers in the hallway. Where was she? Patricia wondered.*

Third person limited (close): *The kitchen was empty. A bare table, no cell phone or book bag. No sneakers to trip on in the hall. Where was she?*

In this second version, we've removed "Patricia glanced," and simply put the reader into Patricia's mind, much as we would with first person. Then, rather than *Where was she? Patricia wondered,* which is removed from Patricia, we used, *Where was she?*

By taking out "Patricia wondered"—language that distances the reader from the character—we remain in her head and simply show what wasn't there (sneakers in the hall) followed by what we know is Patricia's thought.

The advantage with third person limited (close) is the intimacy and immediacy of the writing. This works well for certain genres such as suspense and action/adventure. It's less useful for more descriptive writing. There isn't as much leeway for adding in details the character is less aware of, such as including the Craftsman-style house or the car's failing water pump.

One solution to this is that we manipulate how close we are with our viewpoint character, swooping in closer in tense, dramatic moments, removing "glanced," "listened," "heard," and other distancing language, then stepping back when writing quieter or more transitional or descriptive passages.

Here are two paragraphs to show that kind of shift.

Calling out for her daughter, Patricia raced upstairs. It wasn't time to freak out—Kelly might be in her room, using her computer to DM her friends rather than texting on her phone. Maybe she was in the bathroom and would be angry and embarrassed to find her mother chasing her down. But as Patricia reached her daughter's room and found it empty, panic flooded her.

Missing? Not Kelly. Who to call? Outside the cold glass of the window, the view came into sharp focus. The forest in back blocked out the neighbors. No one outside could help.

In the first paragraph, there's a distance from Patricia. We get a description of what Patricia does as she calls out and then races upstairs.

We are told the room is empty, and panic floods her. Then we shift into the second paragraph, where neither the name Patricia nor any pronouns get used, providing the intimacy of being inside Patricia's head just as we would with first person. The language is tense and tight, without any words to separate the reader from Patricia's experiences.

Our ability to vary the closeness of third person limited point of view allows us to combine the expanded description and distance of third person limited with the intimacy and urgency of first person point of view.

Despite that extra flexibility, third person limited (close) may not be the right point of view for every manuscript. A slower moving, more descriptive work may benefit from the distance of the viewpoint character and the ability to keep a tight rein on pace. But for a thriller or suspense, this closeness can be quite effective.

To experiment with the closeness of a third person point of view, take a section of a work in progress and remove any distancing words, such as pronouns and the character's name, along with words like "thought," "felt," or "believed." Instead, use language as if we are inside the character's head, much as with first person. See how it feels. Notice how it changes the pace and rhythm of the language. The beautiful part about rewrites is that if the change doesn't work, we can always revert to an earlier draft or rewrite again to remove problematic sections.

Third Person Limited (Multiple)

Third person limited (multiple) point of view allows for a writer to use third person limited with more than one character as a viewpoint character. When a writer chooses third person limited (multiple), one chapter or section uses one viewpoint character, written in third person limited, and the next chapter or section switches to another viewpoint character, also written in third person limited point of view.

This does not have to impact the choice of protagonist. The manuscript can still have one central character, even if some chapters are written in third person limited (multiple) with a different viewpoint character.

Third person limited (multiple) can be particularly effective when the writer wants to show events outside the protagonist's point of view. Keep in mind, this is not the same as having multiple protagonists or using third person omniscient point of view (which will be defined next). We can use more than one viewpoint character and still have only one main character.

We might want to have most of our chapters with Patricia as the viewpoint character, then write a few with Kelly as the viewpoint character. Patricia remains the protagonist, even if we write a few chapters or sections with Kelly as the viewpoint character. It might look something like this:

Chapter One: Patricia, the viewpoint character of this chapter, comes home to discover her daughter is missing. She raises the alarm and starts to look for her.

Chapter Two: Kelly, the viewpoint character of this chapter, is on a Greyhound bus. We discover that she is on her way to try to find her biological father. This builds a new kind of tension because we want to know if she succeeds, but we also want to know how long it will take Patricia to discover where Kelly has gone and why.

Even though we no longer have the mystery of why Kelly left home, we do have the mystery of whether she will succeed in finding her biological father or have something awful happen to her along the way. We could, for example, build even more tension by having a creepy guy get on the bus and sit down behind Kelly, then not return to Kelly as the viewpoint character for several chapters, leaving readers to wonder what happens to her while we are away.

Consider how tense it would be if Patricia tracks her daughter's cell phone to the Greyhound bus station and manages to get the bus station manager to show her the security video of her daughter getting on the bus. Readers see the creepy guy paying too much attention to Kelly and sitting near her on the bus.

The bus pulls out, and Kelly's cell phone can no longer be traced. The phone goes straight to voice mail and has clearly been shut off.

Tension can be built from readers knowing that Kelly is unaware of the creepy guy, and both the readers and Patricia are fully aware of him, guessing at what he might be up to. Kelly and the creepy guy vanish somewhere along the bus route, which Patricia learns later in the plot.

Because Patricia is the viewpoint character and the protagonist, we can write as many chapters as we want from her perspective before we return to a chapter with Kelly as the viewpoint character. How often to insert a chapter with Kelly as the viewpoint character depends on what we want to show readers. We could include chapters with Kelly as the viewpoint character for almost half the book, just one chapter near the beginning, or any amount in between. We have the flexibility, based on how we want to create tension. If we write more than half the chapters with Kelly as the viewpoint character, we run the risk of having two protagonists, which is possible but complicated. One of the most challenging aspects of multiple protagonists is that readers must be equally invested in both protagonists, with their objectives, obstacles, and stakes at the same level of importance.

Writing in third person limited (multiple) with only one protagonist can be a great device but be aware of the following issues.

First, it's disorienting for the reader to have several most of the chapters from the perspective of just one viewpoint character, then switch to another late in the book. Typically, if a writer wants to use multiple viewpoint characters, it works best to introduce readers to that convention at the beginning, such as having the first chapter with character A as the viewpoint character and the second chapter with character B as the viewpoint character. Even if we don't see another chapter with character B as the viewpoint character for several chapters after that, we have established at the beginning the convention that there will be more than one viewpoint character, which allows readers to understand the rules of the book from the start.

That's not to say there aren't outliers, with books divided at the halfway mark or shifting to a different viewpoint character late in the game, but writers must understand that it can be disorienting to the reader if the rules are changed late in a manuscript. Just as using second person point of view can limit a manuscript's appeal and make it harder to sell, shifting viewpoint characters late in a manuscript can limit its marketability if it turns off agents and editors.

Another caution about using third person limited (multiple) point of view is to be clear when each shift from viewpoint character to viewpoint character takes place. Switching viewpoint characters mid-chapter or within a paragraph can confuse the reader. The safest choice for shifting between viewpoint characters is to switch between chapters.

If a writer wants to shift within a chapter, it will help to use a section break—an extra double-space, no indent for the first line—but the shift will also work better with clarifying language at the beginning of each shift, showing which viewpoint character we are focused on, along with the change in time and place.

For example, if we wanted to write with both Patricia and Kelly as viewpoint characters and wanted to shift within a chapter, we could do something like the following:

Patricia sat down in her daughter's empty room and began to cry.

Four miles away, Kelly took the seat by the window. The Greyhound would leave soon with only a few other passengers onboard. The guy in the black leather jacket came on at the last minute, the one who'd asked if she wanted to join him for a drink. He carefully avoided making eye contact as he passed her and sat down in the next row. Weirdo, Kelly thought. I'm glad he didn't sit next to me.

Notice that there is a physical break between the two paragraphs. The extra space and lack of indent shows readers we have shifted from one scene to the next. "Four miles away" immediately places us in a new location. Lastly, Kelly's name is in the first sentence, showing readers the shift in viewpoint character. This clarifying language keeps readers from being confused about the time, place, and action of the scene.

There are many books written with multiple viewpoint characters using third person limited point of view in a variety of genres. One example is Alice Feeney's thriller *His & Hers*, which shifts back and forth between viewpoint characters Anna Andrews, a reporter, and Detective Jack Harper, as they investigate a murder. Readers have access to both characters' experiences, but in the close personal style of third person limited (multiple), alternating between the two. Neither character is distanced, as they would be if Feeney had written in third person omniscient.

Third Person Omniscient

Third person omniscient is another form of third person point of view. The publishing industry often uses the term "omniscient" by itself and treats it as a separate category for purposes of querying and discussion, but keep in mind, it falls under the umbrella of third person and uses the conventions of he/she/they.

Third person omniscient point of view provides an outside eye on all the characters and the world of the story. The third person omniscient narrator is all-knowing and can relay to the readers any and all information about the characters, including their thoughts and motivations, and all the events of the story. Third person omniscient has the most flexibility for providing information to the reader, but it's also the least intimate, because the events are experienced from a greater distance.

Third person omniscient is often described as a God's eye or bird's eye view. The "voice" of the narration exists outside every character, including the protagonist, even though the narrator can access the thoughts, feelings, and motivations of each character. The outside narrator can describe a character's internal state. The distinction between omniscient point of view versus first person or third person limited is that the characters are not viewpoint characters. The outside narrator, in effect, serves as the viewpoint character, with access to each character.

If we wanted to look at Patricia and Kelly's unfolding story from a third person omniscient point of view, it might look like this:

Patricia walked up the steps of her 1909 Craftsman house in the Beau Arts neighborhood with a sense of dread. Her mother's intuition screamed that Kelly's refusal to answer the phone didn't come from a teenager's carelessness or a simple missed call. Something was wrong.

Two miles away, as Kelly stepped onto the Greyhound bus. A man in a black jacket followed.

In neither of these paragraphs is Patricia or Kelly a viewpoint character; rather, an all-knowing uber eye narrates the scenes. Third person omniscient point of view provides writers with the opportunity to present multiple characters in the same chapter or section, but not—and this is very important—multiple viewpoint characters. The point of view is still singular—an omniscient perspective—but the narrator has access to every character rather than inhabiting one specific character.

Notice that Patricia's thoughts about her intuition are not written from inside her, but rather through an external voice. The narrative voice reveals what she feels and why. Then, as we skip over to Kelly, we are not in Kelly's head as a viewpoint character stepping onto the Greyhound. Instead, we are told about Kelly's experiences from a greater distance.

To rewrite with Patricia as the viewpoint character, it might look like this:

Dread filled Patricia as she sped up her front steps. Something was wrong.

Notice that we have removed the material that Patricia isn't focused on—her neighborhood and the style of her house—and brought her internal thoughts directly into the forefront of her attention.

For Kelly as the viewpoint character, we might write something like this:

Kelly walked toward the back of the Greyhound, hoping for a seat to herself by a window and no creepy guy across the aisle.

Here we have popped into a teenage voice as she is the viewpoint character. In the industry, we consider the narrator in third person limited to be "absent," and the focus is on the voice of the viewpoint character. With third person omniscient, the narrator has a consistent voice regardless of which character they focus on, especially in the prose. Dialogue remains unique to each character, but description and action is in the narrator or author voice.

Third person omniscient has fallen out of favor in general fiction. Though there continue to be successful bestselling books written in this point of view, it's tricky to do well. Writers working in third person omniscient point of view tend to drift into third person limited, popping into the viewpoint of a specific character's thoughts and experiences, then pulling back for the omniscient narration, then popping back into the viewpoint of another character.

In the industry, we call that "head-hopping," and it's not an effective way to show story. Head-hopping can be disorienting for the reader because it muddies the viewpoint through which the story is told. Consider the following:

Dread filled Patricia as she sped up her front steps. Something was wrong. The bus was crowded and smelled of cigarettes and sweat. Kelly took a seat by the window.

I've exaggerated the issue by having the viewpoint characters switch places mid-paragraph, but the glitch comes when we shift from Patricia as the viewpoint character to Kelly as the viewpoint character rather than presenting both of their experiences from an outside perspective.

To rewrite these lines in third person omniscient point of view, it might look like this:

Patricia sped up the front steps, filled with dread. Something was wrong; she could feel it. Not far away, the bus was crowded and smelled of cigarettes and sweat. Kelly slid in next to the window, grateful for the open seat.

This is third person omniscient point of view, not third person limited, because we learn about more than one character and provide language to show the shift between them. "Not far away" shows readers that we are leaving Patricia and moving over to another character. Then we identify Kelly by using her name, but we do not hop into Kelly's head, so she is never the viewpoint character.

Point of view errors are one of the most common mistakes editors find in manuscripts. It's easy to pop a line in as if another character is the viewpoint character without noticing the head-hopping. It's also easy to shift in and out of first person and third person limited without meaning to, such as starting with I, then shifting into he/she/they.

Head-hopping can be an issue for any point of view. It occurs when we have grounded readers in a specific viewpoint character but hop into another in a confusing manner.

Choosing a viewpoint character and the point of view for a story is one of the most important decisions a writer makes. That choice determines everything about how a reader discovers information. Again, there is no right or wrong choice, only what's best for a specific project.

I'm often asked how a writer can know if they have made the strongest choice for their viewpoint character and point of view. My suggestion is to take a section of a work in progress and try out other viewpoint characters and points of view to see how each one feels.

For Exercise 4, we're going to do just that. This exercise will work whether using an existing draft or the material generated from the first three exercises in this guide.

Exercise 4: Playing with POV

Building on the information generated from Exercise 3, let's assess the point of view and the viewpoint character in a work in progress. This exercise is broken into two options, the first for working with an existing manuscript, the second if starting from scratch with material generated from the previous exercises.

Existing Manuscript

Step One: Take the first chapter or scene of the current draft and keep the current viewpoint character, but rewrite in each point of view. Make sure to rewrite in first person, second person, third person limited, third person limited (close), and third person omniscient. If the current point of view is unclear, that's okay; just step through each point of view and make sure not to hop around between characters within a single rewrite.

It may feel pointless to rewrite in second person point of view, as that's an unlikely choice, but there are two good reasons for including second person in the exercise.

First, we never know what can be learned about the story and the characters unless we explore, and second person will provide a completely different picture, which might teach us something useful.

Second, it can help clarify how much changing point of view impacts a scene. By rewriting in second person point of view, we can see how much that changes the material. The shift can be less obvious between other points of view, such as third person limited and third person limited (close), so playing with second person can help clarify what a shift in point of view truly delivers. With that knowledge, we may be better able to identify the nuanced changes among other points of view.

Step Two: Let the rewrites sit for a day or two, and then come back and reread them. It can be useful to print out the scenes and read them on the page or send them to an e-reader to help create distance from the material on the computer screen.

Which feels right? Which feels authentic to the work? Which flows best?

In my experience, writers have good instincts for what point of view best suits their manuscript. If there is a point of view issue, it's more often because a writer hasn't considered using another point of view. Once exposed to different options, the writer ultimately makes the strongest choice for the project.

Step Three: If the point of view as originally written feels the most authentic, that's great. The right choice had already been made, but new information was likely generated about plot, story, or character.

If a different point of view feels like a better fit, the final step of the exercise is to rewrite the entire project from the new point of view.

New Project

Step One: Write a scene with the character(s) generated in the first three exercises. Don't worry if it's the beginning, middle, or end. Just have fun. See what point of view comes naturally. This may be a place to write that opening scene as described in Exercise Two.

Step Two: After writing the scene, confirm it remains fully in one point of view. Whether first, second, third person limited, third person limited (close), or third person omniscient, carefully assess that the material doesn't slip into another point of view. If it hops around, rewrite until it remains in one point of view.

Step Three: Rewrite the scene in each point of view. Make sure to rewrite in first person, second person, third person limited, third person limited (close), and third person omniscient.

As mentioned previously, it may feel pointless to rewrite in second person point of view, as that's an unlikely choice, but there are good reasons for including it in this exercise.

First, we never know what can be learned about the story and the characters unless we explore, and second person will provide a completely different picture, which might teach us something useful.

Second, it can help clarify how much changing the point of view impacts a scene. By rewriting in second person point of view, we can see how much that changes the material. The shift can be less obvious between other point of views, such as third person limited and third person limited (close), so playing with second person can help clarify what a shift in point of view truly delivers. With that knowledge, we may be better able to identify the nuanced changes among other points of view.

Step Four: Let the rewrites sit for a day or two, and then come back and reread them. It can be useful to print out the scenes and read on the page or send them to an e-reader to help create distance from the material on the computer screen.

Step Five: If the original point of view feels like the right fit, that's great. The right choice had already been made, but see what new information about plot, story, or character came from the exercise of writing the other points of view. If the original point of view isn't a good fit, choose the one that feels best for moving forward with future scenes.

It may be useful to do this exercise again after generating more material. Going back through the exercises more than once will be beneficial to creating a solid first draft.

| 4 |

Objectives, Obstacles, and Stakes Build Character Arc

> Characters want something, which drives their behavior as they fight obstacles. That creates conflict. Without conflict, there's no story.

Writing is subjective. What readers respond to is also subjective. There are no guarantees that years of hard work will pay off in a manuscript that an agent, publisher, or reader will care about.

But there are ways to improve the potential for a successful project.

One of the best ways to make a character engaging and a manuscript more appealing is to give that character clear objectives, obstacles, and stakes. When a character strives for something, overcomes obstacles, then either succeeds or fails to achieve that goal, with something at stake, we have what we call a character arc. The character goes on a journey, which the reader will want to discover.

Building characters without objectives, obstacles, and stakes is also one of the biggest mistakes a writer can make because it builds a character that doesn't matter to readers and doesn't actively change.

The objectives, obstacles, and stakes for a character—especially the protagonist—are a large part of what makes readers continue reading, whether that reader is an agent deciding if they want to represent a manuscript, an editor considering whether to acquire the manuscript for publication, or after the book is published, a reader deciding whether to purchase it or leave a good review.

Another reason that objectives matter is that when a character's objectives are in opposition to those of another character, conflict arises. Readers want to see characters fight for something, whether the battle is internal or external or both. At the heart of every story is conflict.

If a character has a goal, something big stands in the way of achieving that goal, and the cost to the character is high if they don't achieve that goal, readers will want to know what happens next. That translates into turning another page or reading another chapter and investing further into a character.

Even more important are characters with super-objectives. Super-objectives drive the entire plot. The super-objective relates to objectives, obstacles, and stakes, but we are going to isolate each of these concepts to clarify what they are and how to use them to benefit our work and build successful and satisfying character arcs.

Objectives

An objective is a goal. Every character has a goal in every scene. Whether a protagonist wants to take down a bomb-setting super villain or a waitress needs to carry a plate of food to a table without spilling maple syrup down a diner's suit, every character has a goal.

It's true the bomb-setting super villain scenario is more "important" in the sense of greater far-reaching consequences and immediate physical danger. But consider this for our fictional character Patricia: She's a single mom, putting herself through school and working the graveyard shift at a twenty-four-hour diner. If she gets one more complaint from a patron, she'll get fired. Her goal not to spill maple syrup on a diner has just become a lot more important. That's because we have created stakes to go along with her objective. An objective without stakes won't be as important to readers as an objective that will impact the character in a meaningful way.

Goals drive character behavior just like they drive our behavior in the real world. We walk through life with goals in mind, even when we aren't aware of them. Reading this book is likely a result of the goal to finish a rough draft, improve writing skills, or polish a manuscript. Writing a manuscript is typically done with the goal of getting published or the more immediate goal of landing an agent on the road to publication. Publishing a book has its own set of goals, such as money, fame, or a sense of achievement—or just the chance to walk into a local library and see our title on the shelf.

Characters without goals can feel unfocused, pointless, and less engaging than those who do, so building a character's goals into each scene makes their behavior more exciting and understandable and increases the odds that readers will connect. It's also why a less important character can take center stage at times. If that character has a clear goal, readers connect—regardless of that character's place in the larger landscape of the story. This is also true for memoirists writing their own story or narrative nonfiction writers focusing on a real person's experiences. Goals matter.

Consider the following example:

Patricia arrived home and went upstairs to change clothes. She took off her waitress uniform, stuffed it into the hamper, and pulled on a pair of sweatpants and an old sweater. Then she decided the laundry needed to get done, so she loaded up her basket and went into the laundry room. She got a load going before heading downstairs for a snack.

Arriving in the kitchen, she noticed that Kelly wasn't in her usual after-school spot working on her homework.

"Kelly?" she called up the stairs. "Are you in your room?"

After a moment of silence, she trudged up the stairs to knock on Kelly's door.

In this section, Patricia doesn't have any clear goals. Yes, she's getting undressed, but we don't really know why other than work is over. She's doing laundry, but we don't know why other than it needs to be done. There's no tension, and no real reason to keep reading. It might feel like it's the choice of actions that are the problem, but we could rewrite this scene, keeping the exact same actions, and still build in clear objectives. This will make Patricia more engaging.

Patricia's uniform stank of stale sweat. She couldn't wait to get it off and into the sink before the spilled coffee stain set and she had to buy another out of her own money. The full hamper showed that she had yet another task to finish before she could be done for the day. Kelly would be out of clean underwear if she didn't get at least a load of whites done.

Her stomach rumbled as she stuffed the clothes into the washer. She hadn't eaten all day, and she felt lightheaded. Reaching the kitchen, she noticed that Kelly wasn't in her usual after-school spot working on her homework. Anxiety touched the back of her neck. Exhausted but worried, she trudged back upstairs to knock on Kelly's door.

In this example, Patricia does the exact same actions—she comes home, changes clothes, starts her laundry, goes down to the kitchen for a snack, notices her daughter is missing, and goes back up to her room to knock. But now we've included goals. Her shirt stinks, so her objective of getting it off is more important than it was when all we knew was that she was finished with work. Then we learn that if her work shirt is stained, she has to replace it and pay for it herself. That's a much different goal. Patricia's goal is now to keep from losing money on her work shirt. Added to that, she has the goal of keeping her daughter in clean underwear, and we have a clear objective for doing laundry. That's a goal many of us can relate to, even if we aren't going to be charged for a work uniform or don't have children. We have all been in a situation where a household chore is more than just something we should do for ourselves—it's something we should do for another person.

Patricia doesn't just go downstairs for a snack; she's hungry enough to feel ill, so her objective to get something to eat matters a lot more than it did in the first example. And we end the short scene with anxiety about her daughter's well-being. Patricia heads back upstairs to confirm her daughter is all right, not just to see if she's there.

The actions are the same as in the first example, but the clarity of her goals makes it much more compelling to watch those same events unfold. The language is also more specific and colorful, which comes in part because the goals are clearer. Clearer language, clearer goals. Clearer goals, clearer language. That cycle improves the writing as we continue to identify what Patricia is after and why.

Super-objectives

The primary difference between an objective and a super-objective is importance and function within the overall plot. An objective drives a scene. A super-objective drives the entire plot.

Characters have objectives in each scene, such as Patricia's objective to wash her work shirt, but they also have a compelling super-objective that runs through the entire story.

Further, objectives often work in service to the super-objective.

For example, if Patricia's super-objective is to provide a better life for her daughter, keeping her work shirt clean and not losing money replacing it are connected to her desire to build a better environment for Kelly.

If Patricia's super-objective is to become a famous Instagram influencer, having a clean work shirt doesn't relate. Instead, her objective in the previous scene might be to figure out the right outfit for a selfie, not to get her laundry done for work.

Finding a single super-objective to propel a character through a manuscript is key to building an active and engaging character. When agents and editors ask what a character wants, they aren't interested in the objectives of a single scene; they want to know what is at the heart of this character's desires. These are big, sweeping goals, such as catching a killer, dying with grace, or finding a missing teenage daughter.

Super-objectives are also either internal or external. These internal and external super-objectives typically work together as different aspects of the same goal.

An external super-objective is a goal the outside world can watch a character reach for. With Patricia, the goal to find her missing daughter could be an external goal. People know Kelly is missing, and they can see the actions Patricia takes to try to find her.

Patricia's internal goal might be to prove she's worthy of being a parent. Or it could be that she wants to be a better parent than her own mother. Those goals can be invisible to the outside eye. They are connected to finding her daughter, but the police and friends and neighbors can't know Patricia's internal goal unless she tells them.

When identifying a character's super-objective, it's extremely useful to spell out both the internal and external aspects. The strongest choice is to have one of each, related to each other, which drive the character from start to finish. That will help make a more complex character because their actions are driven not just by the super-objective the world can see, but also an internal driver that is psychological and hidden.

A character may or may not be aware of their super-objectives, especially at the beginning. It's also not unusual to have an external goal be clear to everyone, but an internal goal remains hidden, even to the character herself, until the end. For example, a homicide detective searching for a killer is an external goal, but the detective proving they are still able to do their job despite a physical ailment is an internal goal. Both goals drive the detective to solve the homicide, but the detective may be unaware of the internal goal until it's achieved (or not achieved).

Another example would be a warrior trying to win a battle. This is an external super-objective. The internal super-objective could be returning honor to the family or breaking free from a caste system. Perhaps the warrior wants to put down her sword and live in peace but can only achieve that goal after winning a specific battle. The outside world sees her leading the charge against the enemy as she always has, but internally, she's counting on her success to allow her to retire. That makes her internal super-objective connected to her external one, but they work in tandem rather than as carbon copies of each other.

Internal and external super-objectives can also conflict with each other. Take our warrior who wants to retire. It may be that she no longer has the fortitude to kill another human being. Now she's faced with having to kill again before she can put down her sword for good. That creates intense conflict within her psyche as she does something the outside world expects of her, as opposed to living a life of her own choosing and going against expectations. It is her struggle to achieve her internal super-objective that creates her character arc. While external super-objectives also help build a character arc, the character's complete journey is more authentic when the internal super-objective is ultimately either achieved or not.

Obstacles

To make objectives important, characters need obstacles. Something must get in the way of a character achieving their goals, whether that's within a scene or throughout the entire story in opposition to the super-objective.

Without obstacles, goals aren't as important. We don't read stories to watch characters succeed; we read stories to watch characters struggle. It is that struggle, that conflict, which creates drama and draws us through a story as we wait to see if a character achieves what they want.

The larger the obstacle, the more engaged we become with a character. Larger obstacles also create a more complex journey and satisfying character arc as we watch them change and grow.

Obstacles can be physical, psychological, or emotional. Each of these has their own set of problems. Further, an obstacle can be a combination of physical, psychological, or emotional. For example, if a detective faces an armed killer in a shootout, that's primarily physical, but it will also have psychological and emotional aspects. The physical obstacle could be the armed opponent; the psychological obstacle might be a lack of self-esteem in the detective's ability to succeed in a fight; and the emotional obstacle might be fear, which could cause the detective to freeze.

A character losing a romantic relationship likely faces a primarily emotional set of obstacles, but consider a scene where the character fights with the person they love. Let's call the character Tom. He sees his lover with another man, locked in a passionate embrace. Tom could have a psychological fear of conflict, which would be an obstacle to approaching his lover and standing up for their relationship. He could have an emotional breakdown, creating an obstacle to addressing the problem in the moment. Lastly, he could have a physical obstacle if the other guy is much bigger than he is, making Tom afraid to prompt a physical confrontation.

Patricia could have several obstacles in the way of her goals in our short scene. She has the goal of a clean uniform; the obstacle is that it's dirty. She has a goal of not paying for a damaged shirt; the obstacle is that the spilled coffee could leave a stain. She has a goal of being done working for the day; the obstacle is the clean laundry that both she and her daughter need. She has a goal of being satiated; the obstacle is that she hasn't eaten, and we don't know if there is any food in the house. Most importantly, Patricia has a goal of knowing her daughter is safe, and if Kelly has vanished from the house, her absence is an obstacle to that goal.

Many of Patricia's objectives have clear obstacles.

Her super-objective also has obstacles.

If Patricia's internal super-objective is to be a successful single mom, having her daughter run away from home—not to mention kidnapped, injured, or dead—is a huge obstacle. The objective of the scene is to find out if Kelly is home, but that objective plays into the larger super-objective of being a successful mother.

The more writers can identify and enhance character goals in each scene, the stronger that character's actions and motivations will be, and the more readers will connect to them.

Stakes

Stakes are related to objectives and obstacles. Not only does a character need a goal that has obstacles, but the goal has to matter to the character so that it matters to the readers.

If a character doesn't care about a goal, why would a reader?

Consider this goal: Patricia wants a clean uniform. The obstacle could be that it has a coffee stain. If there is no repercussion to her not getting the stain out, the goal doesn't feel very important. By adding in that she might have to pay for the uniform if it won't come clean, we add a stake. But consider what would happen if we made the stakes a little higher.

What if her boss told her that if she damages any more uniforms, she's going to lose her job?

The objective and the obstacle remain the same, but the stakes are higher. If we know she could lose her job if the uniform doesn't come clean, we are now invested in the success of that load of laundry.

By manipulating stakes, we can make events more important to both characters and readers. This is true for objectives in scenes and super-objectives for the entire manuscript. Building higher stakes for individual objectives automatically increases the stakes for the character overall, especially when we link individual objectives with super-objectives.

If Patricia's external goal when she discovers Kelly is missing is to find her daughter, her first action might be to call Kelly's cell phone. If we have Patricia reach her daughter, and her daughter explains where she is and reassures her mother that she's fine, we drop the stakes. If, however, Patricia calls her daughter and it goes straight to voice mail, we have upped her anxiety by raising the stakes. We could amp them up even higher by having her call her daughter and hear the cell phone ring in Kelly's bedroom. Patricia discovers that not only is Kelly missing, but her cell phone has been left behind. The external super-objective remains the same—find Kelly—but the obstacles and stakes are higher.

Exercise 5: Identify the Protagonist's Super-objectives

It's often easy to identify a character's objectives in each scene. Those are typically smaller and more clear-cut than a super-objective. It's much more challenging to identify the single internal and external super-objectives that drive the character from start to finish. But identifying the internal and external super-objectives is key to building the most complex and satisfying characters. It's also important in building a solid plot with each scene important to the story.

Another way to think about the protagonist's internal and external super-objectives is to combine them into a single sentence. For example, Patricia's external super-objective might be to find her daughter. Her internal super-objective might be to act as a responsible single parent. Combining the two into a single sentence might look like this: Patricia searches for her daughter to prove to herself that she is capable of being a responsible single parent.

Notice this has started to sound a lot like an elevator pitch, a short description used to entice an agent or editor to read a full manuscript. That's because an elevator pitch focuses on the intrinsic super-objectives of the character.

This exercise will help identify the internal and external super-objectives, then combine them in a single sentence to describe the heart of the project. Additionally, knowing the internal and external super-objectives, and whether or not the character achieves them, helps to illuminate the character's arc. They start the manuscript wanting something, even if they aren't aware of it. By the end, they have either achieved it or not. That journey creates their arc.

This exercise is in two parts, the first for an existing manuscript, the second for a new project generated through using this guidebook. While the two parts are similar, the steps for a new project are designed to help invent material, whereas the steps for an existing manuscript assume characters are already under development. For stories with more than one protagonist, do this exercise for each one.

Existing Manuscript

Step One: What do other characters believe to be the protagonist's goal? Write this goal out. Don't forget to consider what other characters believe by the end of the manuscript, not just at the beginning. If each character has a different idea of what the protagonist's goal is, is that because the actions of the protagonist are unclear? Or because there aren't any close friends, relatives, or characters in the story who are aware of the protagonist's situation? If the writer doesn't know what the super-objective is, or if it isn't made clear in the writing, identify why it's not clear. If the protagonist's actions are never clear to outsiders, that may point to issues in the manuscript or an author unaware of their protagonist's true motivations.

If there are no other close characters, and that suits the project, invent an outside narrator for the purposes of this exercise. How would an external observer describe the protagonist's primary goal?

Consider this example from our story about Patricia: Patricia searches for her daughter by talking to the police, Kelly's friends, and other people in the community, actions which are visible to outsiders. Outside characters would say Patricia's goal is to find her daughter.

Step Two: By the end of the manuscript, what is the protagonist aware of having accomplished? Write this out. If this isn't clear to the protagonist, that might be something to clarify in the manuscript. By the end of a story, the protagonist would likely be aware of what they have achieved (or not achieved), even if they aren't completely aware of how it impacts other characters.

Consider this example from our story about Patricia: Patricia finds her daughter, saving Kelly from becoming a victim of human trafficking. That would be a clear accomplishment.

Step Three: How does the protagonist feel about their accomplishment? (Or failure?) Write out the answer.

Consider this example from our story about Patricia: Patricia realizes she is a good mother, even in the face of the worst adversity.

Step Four: Combine the information from the first three steps into a single sentence.

Consider this example from our story about Patricia: Patricia overcomes her fear in raising her daughter alone when she saves Kelly from a human trafficking ring.

Step Five: Print or write out that sentence and post it where it's visible. It can be useful to keep what lies at the heart of a story front and center. Continue to revisit that sentence throughout the writing process. By the time the manuscript is polished, the elevator pitch is ready for the query process.

New Project

Step One: What do other characters believe the protagonist's goal to be? Play around with some possibilities—do freewrites and imagine scenarios. Don't worry about whether it becomes the actual super-objective. Don't even worry about whether the other characters invented for this exercise show up in the final draft. Use an imaginary best friend, parent, neighbor, co-worker, or anyone the protagonist might interact with. This is a great time to bring in the creative child.

The goal with this exercise is to have a potential super-objective to draw the protagonist through a first draft of a new manuscript.

Write this goal out.

Consider this example from our story about Patricia: Patricia searches for her daughter by talking to the police, Kelly's friends, and other people in the community, all of which are visible to outsiders. Outside characters would say Patricia's goal is to find her daughter.

Step Two: At the end of the manuscript, what will the protagonist be aware of achieving? By the end, the protagonist will likely be aware of what they have achieved (or not achieved), even if they aren't completely aware of how it impacts other characters.

Consider this example from our story about Patricia: Patricia finds her daughter, saving Kelly from becoming a victim of human trafficking. That would be a clear accomplishment. And it will be much easier to write a first draft knowing what the throughline of the story is. A throughline is the path the story takes, with scenes serving as markers along the way. To learn more about throughlines, read *The Foundation of Plot.*

Step Three: How does the protagonist feel about their accomplishment? (Or failure?)

Consider this example from our story about Patricia: Patricia realizes she is a good mother, even in the face of the worst adversity. Knowing the outcome of Patricia's story can help finish a first draft.

Step Four: Combine the information from the first three steps into a single sentence.

Consider this example from our story about Patricia: Patricia overcomes her fear of failure in raising her daughter alone when she saves Kelly from a human trafficking ring.

Step Five: Print or write out that sentence and post it where it's visible. It can be useful to keep what lies at the heart of a story front and center. Continue to rewrite that sentence as the manuscript develops. It will likely change and strengthen throughout writing the first and subsequent drafts, but each draft of the sentence will help guide each draft of the manuscript. By the time the manuscript is polished, the elevator pitch is ready for the query process.

| 5 |

Emotional, Psychological, and Physical Landscapes

> Characters have internal maps which help writers find their way to complex dynamics and an authentic voice.

Alandscape is the geography of a specific area. It's how a region appears or feels in its totality. The landscape of England is pretty. The landscape of the Swiss Alps is majestic. They are both wonderful—just different.

Characters also have landscapes: emotional, psychological, and physical. A writer can use those landscapes to heighten tension, increase stakes, and engage readers. But first, a writer must understand those landscapes.

Let's start by defining emotional versus psychological landscapes. Keep in mind, I'm using these terms to help you understand character; I am not a psychologist, and I can't help you overcome your fear of snakes, but I do know a lot about what makes a character tick.

Think of emotional versus psychological landscapes in the same way we compare weather and climate.

Weather would mean that it's snowing on my house; it's temporary, just as an emotion is current and fleeting. Climate, in contrast, is a set of long-term conditions, just as one's psychological landscape is long-term and fundamental.

My feeling happy about a five-star review on Amazon is temporary because it is part of an emotional landscape. My ability to keep writing regardless of bad reviews is long-term because it is based on my psychological landscape.

Emotional Landscapes

A character's emotional landscape can be further explored based on either their emotional journey through the entire manuscript or their immediate emotion in a specific scene.

While a character's short-term emotional landscape will be dictated, in part, by their long-term mental health and how well equipped they are psychologically to handle situations, the interaction of those states will evolve during rewrites. In other words, if a character overreacts in a scene, let that emotional state unfold throughout the draft rather than assuming there's no reason for that overreaction and cutting it without exploration. During rewrites, analyze the scene and determine what is in the character's psychological makeup to cause their overreaction, and then determine if it's justified. This can allow for a more complex emotional landscape with bigger peaks and valleys and a more dynamic and interesting character.

We can also develop a character's psychological landscape in advance, and let that help guide emotional reactions during a specific scene.

Regardless of which way we work (letting the emotional landscape show the psychological landscape or letting the psychological landscape inform the emotional), the two landscapes will feed into each other and help create a more authentic character.

To imagine a character's emotional landscape, it can be useful to start at the opening pages and identify the character's "world before." World before is the state a character is in before the first scene in a manuscript. It is often called the "stasis," which means an unchanging condition. An event at the beginning of the manuscript breaks the stasis of the character and sends them in a new direction, launching the manuscript. The character may be happy, sad, scared, or angry; there's no right or wrong place for your character to start from. Just consider when their emotional state begins to change. That change can be abrupt—for example if their romantic partner dies—or gradual, as they slowly realize they are in love with the girl next door.

Once we identify the emotional state of a character in the world before, we can track their emotional state going into each event. Then we can find ways to break that emotional state.

Readers want to see characters who are active. To be emotionally active requires change. One way to achieve change is by showing the emotional landscape in a state of flux. If a character is happy, find ways to make them sad. If a character is terrified, find ways to calm them down; their fear can always ramp up again later.

The degree to which we want characters to exhibit emotional states will depend, in part, on genre, but any manuscript can benefit from a character who exhibits a changing emotional landscape.

Let characters experience a wide range of emotions, even if they don't always show those emotions to other characters. In the Star Trek franchise, Spock was a fascinating character because he occasionally broke from his stoic Vulcan emotional state. But he was also interesting because he provided a calm juxtaposition for the other characters having big emotions around him. Westerns thrive on those stoic characters. But even though we often like stoic characters, we don't want all the characters in a story to withhold their emotions. If we are inside a stoic character, their internal emotional landscape might look very different than what they show to the outside world. If no one shows strong emotions, a manuscript can feel flat. Conversely, if everyone shows the same emotions or emotions to the same degree, no single character's emotional state is important.

Secondary characters can be useful to highlight a main character's emotional state. If the protagonist is calm, let other characters be hysterical. If the protagonist is furious, let another character refuse to engage. If the main character is happy, we can see that more clearly in comparison to characters who are not.

Building Emotions

Emotions are an immediate reaction to events or situations. We feel happy when something good happens. We feel sad when something bad happens. We can experience hopelessness when our current situation feels suffocating and unchangeable. But each of these examples is short-term. The length of time we feel happy about something good happening is finite. Winning an award feels great in the moment; the next day, we might feel hollow because the "high" of the event has passed. Our sorrow over a bad event will also fade away. It may be quick, such as recovering from bad news about someone else, or slow, such as recovering from a serious personal setback, but the sadness prompted by an event will eventually fade. Even grief becomes blunted over time.

Do not confuse negative emotional states with depression, which would be part of a character's psychological state. Even people with depression can feel happiness over a good event, but their return to sadness likely happens faster. Further, the degree to which they experience happiness may be less, and they may not enjoy that moment of happiness in the same way as a person who doesn't suffer from depression.

By assessing the character's emotional state at the beginning of the manuscript, we can determine their short-term reactions. With the start of the first scene, we can determine the degree of change the character experiences because of each event moving forward. Showing the character's emotional state at the beginning of a manuscript can provide a baseline for the character's landscape. It allows for the reader to know how the character feels before the next event happens, then see how they respond to that event. This immediately reveals a lot about the character. We see if they take things in stride, blow up, or respond with fear, anger, excitement, or any other specific emotion.

Regardless of the genre, the emotional landscape we build for a character—or real person if it's memoir or narrative nonfiction, as real people have emotional landscapes, too—sets the tone for the entire manuscript. How readers initially feel about a character is largely dependent on the character's emotional state. We respond to the emotions of others, both in real life and on the page.

Psychological Landscape

While emotions are impacted by everything in a character's environment, a character's psychology—a complex combination of biology, genetics, and experiences—is a driving force behind behavior, and much more permanent than an emotion.

A character's underlying psychology greatly impacts their actions. Psychology determines a character's ability to handle events as well as how they might respond to any situation. The actions of characters create events, and events build plot. A character's psychological landscape is fundamental to developing a plot.

An individual's place on the positivity spectrum is an important aspect of their psychology. Human beings likely come into the world with a baseline of positivity. We all know those upbeat people who see the best in a situation and those who consistently find their glass half full. Studies show the inclination for positivity may be set up so early in life that babies could be born with a predisposition for a positive or negative baseline. Positivity is a continuum, and our characters fall somewhere on that spectrum. Their place on that line will dictate a lot about how they approach situations.

We can also think about our characters from basic personality traits.

Are they outgoing or shy? Trusting or suspicious? Talkative or taciturn? Organized or chaotic?

One of my favorite descriptions of the contrast between A- and Z-type personalities is this: A-type always puts the cap back on a tube of toothpaste. Z-type have already lost it behind the toilet.

Obviously, these dichotomies don't consistently apply to everyone, and their place on any continuum can be dictated in part by a given situation. Just like the continuum of positive to negative, these characteristics are all spectrums. But characters fall on these lines, and those positions impact behavior—everything from how comfortable they are in a crowd to how detailed and specific their life goals are. These aspects of personality are likely innate, and the character can do little to change them, but they can learn to adjust their behavior in reaction to events and make choices in their life that support their personality type. Knowing these aspects of a character's personality can help us understand not just how they will act in any given situation but why.

Psychological components are also driven by experience and environment. How a child is treated growing up can exaggerate any of their innate traits. Events, whether traumatic or positive, can cause permanent behavioral shifts in a character's evolution. For example, a child who was bitten by a dog may continue to have anxiety around dogs. Similarly, a child who has never had a dog may have anxiety around dogs, but the triggers are quite different. A child who has a lot of experience with animals may only fear a dog that's the same breed as the one that bit them, whereas the child who never interacted with animals may be afraid of all dogs.

Different experiences and environments can also dictate an adult's behavior. As an example, let's create a character named Jim. He loves dogs, owns dogs, and casually interacts with dogs, but when he sees a German shepherd like the one who bit him when he was a kid, his heart rate bumps up and his palms start to sweat. He feels intense anxiety. He gives the dog—and its owner—a wide berth.

For a second example, let's call our character Cynthia. She did not grow up interacting with dogs and feels anxious around all dogs. Because of this, she might avoid places where she could run into one. She might choose not to visit friends in their homes if they are dog owners and would be less likely to get romantically involved with a dog owner.

This kind of background information can help build tension for our characters. A romance where one person has a dog, but the romantic interest is afraid of dogs, provides fodder for conflict. Why the person is afraid of dogs will determine how they act and how the plot unfolds. Jim will either have to overcome his fear or beg the romantic partner to get another kind of dog after their current German shepherd dies of old age. Cynthia will have to learn to embrace dogs, starting with the one her romantic partner owns.

Both characters have obstacles created by dogs, but they deal with the situations differently. Jim has to overcome his fear of a specific dog breed, so he might interact with the specific breed that scares him. Cynthia has to learn what dogs are like, so she might interact with any dog to overcome her anxiety. These situations set up a different series of events. Jim doesn't need to go hang out at the dog park to see a variety of dogs, but Cynthia might. Cynthia doesn't need to seek out German shepherds, but Jim will.

While this is a simple event compared to scenarios such as enduring physical abuse or losing a parent as a young child, the same principles can be applied to any situation.

If the protagonist or other characters have mental health issues, such as depression, psychosis, sociopathy, or OCD, make sure to research those issues well to accurately portray genuine mental health complications. While anyone with a clinical diagnosis will act differently from another person with the same diagnosis, understanding how the condition can impact behavior will make those characters authentic and believable. Writers have a responsibility to treat mental health issues with compassion. Even sociopathic behaviors can have root causes, and understanding those causes can create more interesting characters. No one is all good or all bad. It may be that they only reveal certain characteristics to certain people, but that's useful information for the writer to know as well.

Understanding our characters' psychological landscapes helps to create characters who seek out or avoid certain circumstances and situations. Understanding their backgrounds can make a character's behavior more realistic. We can also use it to heighten anxiety, fear, or other strong emotional reactions to events. Consider the great film character

Indiana Jones, played by Harrison Ford. "Indy" famously feared snakes, so everyone watching the first movie was just waiting for the pit of snakes to appear, not because the snakes were a surprise but because the audience wanted to see how the character dealt with that phobia, which was clearly set up through the character's psychology.

Physical Landscapes

A character's physical landscape can involve both long- and short-term issues. A long-term issue would be something like a chronic illness or a debilitating injury. A short-term issue would be like standing at the edge of a cliff with the character in danger of falling.

Both long- and short-term issues impact a character's behavior, but they play different roles. For example, a person with Multiple Sclerosis chased to the edge of a cliff isn't likely to be thinking about their disease as they try to escape a killer. But a person with Multiple Sclerosis, suffering from vision loss due to a flare-up of their disease will have a harder time getting away from the person trying to kill them. In this scenario, the long-term physical landscape of the character augments the danger to them in the short-term of the scene.

Similarly, a person currently being treated for cancer would likely approach a new romantic relationship differently than a person without a life-threatening disease.

If someone pulls a gun on a character, the character is in physical danger. If someone pulls a gun on the protagonist, and the protagonist uses a wheelchair, that character has different avenues of escape than someone who can easily run, jump, or swim away.

By assessing your character's physical landscape, you can increase the tension in any situation. For example, I wear contacts because my eyesight is terrible. If I were a character in a crime novel, and someone came into my house in the middle of the night, I would struggle to escape without running into something. Even if I managed to grab my glasses off the bedside table, the lenses are so thick, everything appears warped. My "chase" scene would be a harrowing, half-blind dash for safety as if racing through a fun house with everything off-kilter.

If we wanted to increase the danger and tension in a chase scene, we could create a character with vision like mine who gets chased out of their house at night when they aren't wearing their contacts and didn't manage to grab their glasses, which actually makes the situation worse. Long-term physical issues impact everything our characters deal with, making them more human and adding to their complexity. It also provides additional challenges for them to overcome throughout the course of the plot, building more obstacles.

For memoir and narrative nonfiction, while physical limitations can't be invented, remaining cognizant of the physical issues that underly a person's actions and behaviors can help provide a clearer picture of the events that make it to the page.

Exercise 6: Emotional, Psychological, and Physical Landscapes

Building emotional, psychological, and physical landscapes for the protagonist can help build more complex scenes. Obviously, landscapes can be drawn for any character and can be quite useful, but for the purposes of this exercise, let's start with the protagonist.

Step One: For an existing project, develop an emotional landscape for the protagonist. Create a graph or timeline of the character's emotional state throughout the manuscript. One way to accomplish this is to make notes in the margin of every chapter of the character's current emotional state, and identify when it changes. Be very aware of any scene in which their emotional state can't be identified. That might indicate a place to rewrite for greater emotional stakes.

For those working on a brand-new project, identify the character's emotional state at the beginning of the project, and determine their emotional state at the end. Then keep this exercise handy to continue describing the landscape in each chapter while writing the first draft.

Use big emotions such as happy, sad, angry, and afraid. It's okay to be simplistic, as we're just trying to identify big peaks and valleys of emotions, not all the nuances. That can come later during rewrites.

Step Two: Are there peaks and valleys throughout the manuscript? If not, identify places where those emotions can be heightened. Where can a character feel more joy, more fear, more anxiety, or more of whatever emotional state the character is in? Even more importantly, how does the next event change that state?

For those working on building a brand-new character, write each scene with an eye toward the emotional state of the character. Find ways to enhance that state and track it on a graph or timeline.

Step Three: Develop a psychological landscape. This requires analyzing the character's backstory. Identify the character's psychological makeup. Are they confident, outgoing, shy, organized? Build reasons for their traits. Did they have an idyllic childhood, with parents who loved them and supported them, letting them grow into self-assured adults? Or was their childhood fraught with inattentive, abusive, or absent parents, bullying siblings, or overwhelming poverty?

A child who grew up on the street, struggling with homelessness, will have a different psychological landscape than a child who grew up with all the resources of wealthy and attentive parents. But a child with loving parents who grew up experiencing homelessness will also have a different psychological landscape than a child who grew up with all the resources of wealth, but absent parents.

Building a psychological landscape for a character can be very complex. Identify as many nuances and intersections of both positive and negative experiences as possible.

Step Four: Create a physical landscape for the protagonist. Do they have any long-term physical complications? Where can that complication come into play, such as a person with diabetes lacking access to insulin or someone with poor eyesight losing their contacts and glasses?

Where does the character experience short-term physical complications? Characters can face other characters who present danger, such as in a physical fight. Characters can also face natural dangers, such as a storm or a long walk in the dark. And characters can face dangers from potential accidents, such as car crashes, poison, falls, and contact sports. Regardless of genre, characters can have their obstacles and stakes raised with imminent physical danger.

For those working on a new project, invent some potential scenarios where the character can be in physical danger. Every genre can have scenes with characters in physical danger; those scenes don't just exist in thrillers and murder mysteries. A historical is filled with the potential for physical danger, from runaway horses to infections without a cure. A romance could include scenarios such as ex-lovers becoming stalkers, or discovering a current lover is married to a jealous and violent spouse, or joining a new romantic partner in their dangerous hobby. Sci-fi and fantasy is wide open, from well-armed aliens to fire-breathing dragons. Each scenario has the potential to become a scene or chapter.

Step Five: Post the graphs or timelines or other physical representations of each landscape somewhere visible, such as an office wall or organized in a binder. Use these visual aids to help identify where and how the danger—emotional, psychological, and physical—can be increased to build higher stakes. Generating these landscapes can also prompt scenes or additions to scenes. Whether writing a brand-new project or working an existing draft, these can be useful for rewriting or adding material.

| 6 |

Backstory and Exposition

> Readers need some information some of the time,
> not all of the information all of the time.

One aspect of creating character that can be a challenge, especially with a longer project, is to determine how much backstory and exposition a reader requires to understand the story. It's easy to confuse the two terms as they are often combined. But for the purposes of this guide, let's make a distinction.

Backstory is everything that happened to the character throughout their entire life, while exposition is everything that a reader has to know about a character's past because it impacts the present.

Backstory relates to what shaped the character. Exposition relates to a reader's ability to understand the character.

A reader does not need to know everything about a character's history. Even the writer doesn't need to know everything about a character's history, only enough to build a complex character. Writers differ widely in how much backstory they generate for a project. Further, a writer might build a complex backstory for one character in one manuscript, then just use bare outlines for others; it all depends on how the writer works and the needs of a specific project. It's much like writers who outline and writers who work organically, developing the plot on the page. Some writers need backstories written out and detailed, while others use only what they need for each character and the scenes in the manuscript.

Exposition is slightly different. Readers need exposition to help them understand present-day actions. For our purposes, if readers don't need the information, it's backstory. If they do, it's exposition.

Consider the following for Patricia. She graduated from high school with one thousand seniors in her class; this is backstory. One of her classmates was Peter Kincaid, who is now the chief of police in her town; this is exposition.

Here is how that information might play out in a scene:

Patricia sat down on the sofa, trying not to panic. With the instinct of a mama bear, she knew her daughter was in trouble. Calling 911 felt over-the-top, but she wanted to bring in the authorities right away. She'd watched enough true crime to know the first forty-eight hours were critical. She thought about high school. Her graduating class had one thousand students, and she only knew a handful. One of those students was Peter Kincaid, who was now the chief of police. She picked up the phone to call him.

In this example, we can see that knowing her graduating high school class had one thousand students is extraneous to the scene or her actions. But the fact that she has a personal relationship with the chief of police is useful, and readers may want to know that information moving forward, as it impacts Patricia's behavior.

We could also include this material in a subtler way:

Patricia sat down on the sofa, trying not to panic. With the instinct of a mama bear, she knew her daughter was in trouble. Calling 911 felt over-the-top, but she wanted to bring in the authorities immediately. She'd watched enough true crime to know the first forty-eight hours were critical.

Peter.

Her hand shook as she picked up the phone. Would his number even be the same?

"Hello?" His voice hadn't changed since high school. At homecoming, they had danced in the spotlight as king and queen, his crown askew. She'd thought they would live happily ever after.

"I need your help."

"As your ex? Or as the chief of police?"

In this example, we have let the scene show readers the exposition (she was high school sweethearts with Peter, who is now the chief of police) because it's relevant to her current situation (her daughter is missing, and she wants help from the authorities).

Could we have done the scene without the exposition? Sure, she could call the police station and ask to talk to Peter, then they could have had a conversation about her missing daughter without mentioning any background between them, but if we want to use it later, perhaps as a romantic storyline, it would be awkward that we hadn't shared that information with readers during their first interaction.

We could also leave it out of the manuscript altogether, but that doesn't build character as much as it does to include their shared history. By building a complex backstory, with relationships that appear in Patricia's present, we add layers to the situation.

Writers might choose to discover character background as they work on a scene or create backstories to help develop characters before they write; there is no right or wrong way to accomplish this. If we find later that we've added background which doesn't impact the current situation, it may be better to cut that backstory or find a way to turn it into exposition—making it matter in the character's present.

What Readers Need to Know

A common writing challenge is knowing which backstory and exposition information to include. When building a character's history, everything can be useful for the writer, but not everything will be useful for the reader. Knowing specific details about a character's history can add color and round out a reader's understanding of their motivations, but a reader rarely needs more than a sprinkling of backstory in a manuscript.

How much to include varies from manuscript to manuscript, but there are ways to identify what readers do or do not need to know. When writing a scene and including background information, consider what purpose that information serves. Is it just to build the character, or does it relate to the plot? Does it move the story forward or just fill space? Make sure the character's backstory connects to who the character is throughout the manuscript and that it provides more than just color. If it impacts the current situation, it also provides depth and is more likely to move the story forward.

When Readers Need to Know

Another common misstep for writers is providing background information earlier than a reader needs it. Referencing a past event or relationship at the beginning of the manuscript, then not connecting it to the character's present day until one hundred pages later will likely create a "huh?" moment for the reader rather than an "ah ha" moment. Readers can't remember everything they read and won't remember a minor detail if it's too far removed from its introduction. It can be unclear why readers are being told a particular piece of information if its importance isn't revealed until much later in the story.

Using Patricia and her relationship with Peter Kincaid as an example, imagine the following. In one draft, we mention Patricia knew someone named Peter Kincaid on page two. Then, sixty pages later, we have her call the police station and ask for Chief Kincaid, but we don't include the information that he was her boyfriend in high school. Many readers might miss the importance of his name on page two and forget by page sixty. If, however, we mention that he was her boyfriend in high school immediately before she makes the call, readers will understand the complex nature of her reaching out to him without having to spell it out in the call. Readers will be aware of the subtext because of the immediacy of the exposition.

Info Dumps

One of the biggest dangers in dealing with backstory and exposition is the dreaded info dump. An info dump is a long paragraph (or more) of information that the writer drops on the reader in one big, clunky chunk. Info dumps are a problem for multiple reasons.

First, an info dump can feel like an author or narrator intrusion rather than naturally occurring thoughts from the character. An author or narrator intrusion is when the writer breaks into the narrative and provides information without using a character's thoughts, dialogue, or action to function as the method of delivery or by including the information in a clunky, obvious way. As readers, we can feel it when a writer or narrator has shown up on the scene, often on a soapbox, to spoon-feed us information. This can feel condescending because it appears the writer doesn't trust the reader to understand a situation and believes they need to point something out so the reader doesn't miss it or misunderstand it.

The second problem with an info dump is that even if we succeed in doing the dump in the character's or narrator's voice, it could still be awkward and unnecessary to dump so much information on the reader all at one time.

Lastly, an info dump is likely filled with more specific details than the reader needs about any situation.

Consider the following:

Patricia looked around her daughter's room and determined that Kelly was missing. More than a million and a half teenagers run away every year in the United States, and now Kelly had become one of those statistics. Runaways were more likely to engage in risky behavior, use drugs, and commit crimes. She would be at greater risk for sexually transmitted disease, unwanted pregnancy, and not finishing high school. Not to mention that trafficking or forced prostitution at the hands of an older person could also threaten her.

This paragraph is an info dump. It's possible that Patricia knows all these facts, but this is very dry and demonstrates an author or narrator intrusion. We might want readers to have all this information, and we don't trust them to pick it up in other ways, so we dump it on them in one fell swoop.

Even if we believe that Patricia could know all that information, or if a narrator's voice was appropriate for the situation, it is still too much too fast. Consider the following:

Patricia turned Kelly's computer on. Maybe she could find evidence of where her daughter had gone. She tried to get into Kelly's email but found it password protected. Frustrated, she googled "what to do when a child runs away." Several websites popped up, with everything from the statistics of teen runaway pregnancies to the likelihood of mental health issues and drug addictions. Patricia continued scrolling and saw that trafficking numbers were on the rise, and she felt herself start to hyperventilate. Kelly was in danger— she had to do something.

Once again, even though this information comes from Patricia as the viewpoint character, it's still too much information dumped on the reader at one time.

We can sprinkle this information throughout more than one scene. Patricia can worry about drugs in one scene, pregnancy in another, and trafficking in another. Every fear doesn't need to hit her (and the reader) all at one time.

One of the reasons that writers tend to write info dumps is research. We love to research aspects of our works in progress and often find facts and statistics fascinating. And they can be, but that doesn't mean everything we research should end up in our work, and it definitely won't work as well when included in one big chunk. This is true whether an info dump is about a character's backstory or factual information related to the story.

Using Dialogue to Provide Exposition

Suppose we want readers to know that one and a half million children run away in the US every year. We can work that into the manuscript without using an info dump.

Consider the following phone call between Patricia and her ex-boyfriend Peter, now the chief of police:

Patricia felt tears welling up in her eyes, and she struggled to keep her voice steady. "How many kids go missing every year?"

Peter hesitated. She knew it must be staggering if he didn't want to answer. "Just tell me."

"One and a half million."

Patricia sucked in a breath. How could the police find one teenage girl with so many other missing children out there?

"But that doesn't mean we won't find Kelly." Peter's reassurance meant little in the face of Patricia's growing panic.

Notice how we drop just one statistic in, not all the other aspects of teenage runaways. Then, we deliver it to Patricia in dialogue that feels natural. That means the information is delivered naturally to the readers, too. We never have to force-feed information to readers. When worked into prose or dialogue in subtle ways, readers will figure out for themselves what's important.

We usually have more background information in our imaginations than we need on the page. While we will build more complete characters through understanding their backstories, be careful about including too much information, especially in an info dump, or including that information so early that readers miss the importance.

One very useful intentional rewrite can be simply to identify where we have done an info dump or included background information that doesn't move the story forward. Identify any section with too much backstory included in one big chunk or backstory that doesn't connect to the current life of a character.

Exercise 7: Building Character Backstory

Backstory can provide very useful information, even if none of the material appears in the manuscript. Backstory can help determine how a character behaves in the present and why. Use a freewrite to develop backstory, whether in a new project or a work in progress.

Step One: Starting with the protagonist, write a brief history of the character. Include their birthday, parental relationships, siblings, and something about their childhood. There's no right or wrong information to include, but here are a few suggestions:

Who was their first love?

What kind of music did they listen to as a child?

What are they most afraid of?

Who do they idolize?

Where do they like to vacation?

Are they the first to strike up a conversation at a party? Or do they wait until someone strikes up a conversation with them?

What do they do first thing in the morning, and what do they do right before they go to bed?

How are they connected to the other characters in the manuscript? Ask this last question every time a new character appears.

Step Two: Use the biographical material generated in this exercise when writing and rewriting each scene. Consider how the character's history impacts their behavior in the present. This could be a time to rewrite the full work in progress guided by this new information. Otherwise, use it moving forward with new material, then go back later and do an intentional rewrite for how each character's backstory impacts their actions in the present.

| 7 |

Dialogue and Character Voice

It's not what a character says that matters—it's how they say it.

One of the most effective ways to create memorable characters is through their use of dialogue. What we talk about may not be unique, but how we say things can be. If we imbue our characters with regionalisms, different educational backgrounds, jargon, and verbal quirks, word choices can become as recognizable as physical details.

In fact, in a literary context, dialogue can stand out just as much as description. Let's use Patricia as an example. We can describe her in a variety of ways: how she looks, what she wears, her facial expressions, and how she stands, walks, or moves. All of those will help build a picture of a character in a reader's mind, but a single line of dialogue can pop even more.

Consider the following example.

Patricia wore her hair in cornrows, and her skin was flawless, but her eyes were weary from long hours on her feet. She walked into the quiet break room and sat down with a sigh. Jean, the older woman who'd taken Patricia under her wing since the first day, trudged in a moment later.

"My dogs are barking something fierce." Jean dropped into the chair with the crooked leg. It rocked forward, but she rocked it back, a skill they had all mastered. *"You okay? You look rough."*

Patricia debated what to say. *My daughter is missing? Kelly ran away? I'm terrified?* *"Nothing a good night's sleep won't cure."*

Jean raised an eyebrow. *"That all you need?"*

We have a sense of both characters through the combination of physical characteristics, actions, and what they say. We know Patricia isn't being honest. We also know that Jean is someone who looks out for Patricia, so we can gather that Patricia struggles whether to be forthright with her situation or not. Then we see her choose not to share.

Jean shows a clear voice through her dialogue. "My dogs are barking" indicates certain things about her. She's older, she uses colloquialisms, and we can make guesses about her level of education. "That all you need?" shows how she uses grammar, and the casualness between them indicates their level of trust and friendship. It also shows that Jean doesn't believe Patricia and is there to listen when she's ready to talk. We can sense from the exchange that Patricia might benefit from telling Jean the truth.

That's a lot of work accomplished by just a few lines.

How do we build strong dialogue? Do we write how people speak, or make every line perfect? The answer lies somewhere in between. The glorious part of being a writer is that we can write dialogue exactly the way we want it, unlike in the real world, where we often think of the perfect comeback hours after we need it. But to make our characters feel "real," they can't be perfect all the time.

One way to approach dialogue is to make it more important than pedestrian conversation, but also use broken grammar, odd words, slang, and unusual or regional phrases to build authentic speech.

Let's start out with what we don't need to hear characters say.

Hello. How are you? My name is ...

Cut everything banal. Consider the following scene.

Patricia entered the police station. She would report Kelly missing and hope for the best. She walked up to the receptionist. "Hi, my name is Patricia, and I want to report a missing person."

This is better:

Patricia entered the police station and crossed to the receptionist. "My daughter is missing."

By cutting the unnecessary words, we make her line of dialogue stand out. Then, rather than including the rather formal "I want to report a missing person," we add urgency by stating the more important information: *My daughter is missing.*

When writing the first draft of dialogue, it can be helpful just to get words down. Sort out the intent of what the character wants to say, even if it's lacking in nuance. In the industry, we call dialogue that is unimaginative, too literal, or lacking in nuance "on the nose." This means that the character says exactly what they think, with no interesting language and no subtext. There may be moments when characters say exactly what they think, like, "I don't want to go to the party," but most of the time, dialogue is more effective if it's complex. When writing and rewriting, consider the following observations to improve the dialogue:

People rarely say exactly what they mean.

People rarely address each other by name.

People rarely speak with flawless grammar and often use fragments.

Consider this scenario for Patricia. She wants to call her ex-boyfriend from high school. She broke his heart when they were teenagers, and she hasn't talked to him since the day they graduated. He's now the acting chief of police, and she wants his help.

That call could go like this:

Hi, Peter, I know we haven't spoken since I broke your heart in high school, but I need your help. My daughter Kelly is sixteen years old and missing.

That example spells everything out exactly as Patricia thinks and feels. But no one speaks like that. Further, it leaves nothing for the reader to analyze.

A stronger choice might be the following:

"Peter? It's Patricia."

Dead air hangs heavy.

His voice—when it finally comes on the line—was deeper than she remembered. "It's been a long time."

"I'm sorry about that."

"Let me guess. You need my help."

This exchange provides character rather than just a laundry list of information. We see his lack of response when she says her name. When he does respond, it's to acknowledge how long it's been. This provides the background information—the exposition—to readers in a more interesting way than the first example, where Patricia spells it all out for us.

Readers like to be active participants, drawing their own conclusions from the information writers provide. And the more naturally that dialogue flows, the less aware readers are of the artifice of polished dialogue honed through multiple rewrites. It will feel instead as if the character is in the same room, speaking for the very first time, without a rehearsal.

Peter's final line, *"Let me guess. You need my help,"* shows us something about him as a character. He's used to people needing him. He doesn't anticipate that Patricia is calling him up for a date. He's aware that his position and their history most likely mean she has a problem that he's in a position to solve.

Let's see how we might continue the dialogue to add more information about the situation.

"My daughter is missing."

"Age?"

"Sixteen."

"When did you last see her?"

"This morning. I know it hasn't been twenty-four hours yet—"

"We take missing minors very seriously. Can you come to the station? And bring a recent photo?"

His words reassure her at first—a person in a position of authority wants to help. Then the reality sets in. He would only act this fast if Kelly was in real danger.

"On my way."

Again, we aren't going to bring up that Patricia broke Peter's heart in high school; let readers wonder about their relationship and history for a while before we give them the background. One of the best ways to build characters is to create questions in the reader's mind that they need answers to. Dynamics of relationships are often interesting, so don't give away all the details too quickly.

Before we go any further, let's address a mechanical issue that many writers struggle with: how to use dialogue tags.

A dialogue tag—he said, she asked—is used to identify the speaker. There are specific grammatical rules for incorporating tags into dialogue.

Take a look at the structure of the following sentence.

"I appreciate your willingness to help," Patricia said.

Notice the comma at the end of the line of dialogue after the world help, followed by the end quote mark and *Patricia said.* Many writers incorrectly put a period at the end of the sentence before a dialogue tag. However, the period doesn't belong there when it's followed by a dialogue tag because they function as a single unit. Therefore, this example is incorrect: "I appreciate your willingness to help." Patricia said. That would separate the dialogue tag from the line of dialogue.

Typically, it's best to stick to said or asked for the tag; they fade into the background for readers, while words like commented, growled, or shrieked pop out as unnecessary, breaking up the dialogue rather than adding to the scene.

Another common error is using too many dialogue tags. Readers need fewer tags than writers think. If two characters are talking, and they go back and forth, we may not need any tags at all. Especially if action is incorporated to show who speaks a line. Action can often identify a speaker even better than a tag.

Consider the following scene where Peter and Patricia are in the same room:

"Thank you, Peter." Patricia dropped her eyes. "I appreciate your help."

By using an action in place of the dialogue tag, we still identify the speaker, but we also show the reader something about the character. We see Patricia's action, building in more about her behavior and their dynamic, whereas the tag provides no information other than who said the line.

Here's another example of using an action instead of a tag:

Patricia wanted to reach across the desk and touch his hand. "Thank you, Peter." She kept herself in check.

When more than two people are talking, tags are important, indicating which character is responding. But we can also use actions with multiple characters engaged in conversation. This can make the writing feel more active because the words said and asked aren't there as "filler."

Peter shuffled the papers in front of him. "I'll see what I can do."

"Thank you."

A female uniformed officer appeared, tapping a hesitant knock on the doorframe. "Sir, I have that security footage you requested."

Patricia bit the inside of her lip. Would they learn anything from the cameras at the bus station?

"Thank you." Peter held out his hand for the CD.

The patrol officer glanced at Patricia, a question in her eyes and a tight grip on the CD turning her fingers white.

"I'll take it from here." Peter leaned over his desk, his hand still outstretched.

The officer left the room, taking some of the oxygen with her.

"Was it something I said?" Patricia gestured toward the empty doorway.

"No. We just don't usually let civilians into this part of the station."

Notice there isn't a single dialogue tag in this exchange, but there's no question who says what, even with three characters in the room. Further, each action shows us something about the situation, including character relationships (the patrol officer tapping on the doorframe) and the characters' emotional state (Patricia biting her lip, and the patrol officer's tight grip on the CD).

Talking Heads

Talking heads are another common problem with dialogue. Dialogue usually works best when it's broken up by actions, descriptions, or thoughts. Any time more than a few lines of dialogue occur, make sure something breaks them up; otherwise, the dialogue feels unnatural, and the characters can appear flat.

Consider the following example:

"How is your father doing?" Patricia asked.

"Fine. I heard you'd moved to Toledo," Peter said.

"I did, but I moved back home about three years ago," Patricia said.

"What brought you back?" Peter asked.

"I thought it would be a better place to bring up my daughter," Patricia said.

Consider the following example:

Patricia scrambled for something to say. "How is your father doing?"

"Fine." Peter chuckled to himself.

His father had been a tough old guy twenty years ago. Patricia imagined he hadn't changed much.

"I heard you moved to Toledo."

She could imagine what else had been said about her, but she wasn't about to ask. "I did, but I moved back home about three years ago."

"What brought you back?"

A failed marriage, a disastrous career, a need to lick her wounds. "I thought it would be a better place to bring up my daughter."

The first version is correctly tagged but not very interesting, and the bulk of the tags are unnecessary. The second version fills out the event. We can see Patricia struggling to connect with her ex. We learn something about both Peter and his father, including how Patricia sees them. Then, we learn a lot about Patricia's background, but that exposition is neatly dropped in through the context of the dialogue, so it feels natural in how it's provided. And there's not a single dialogue tag in the entire exchange.

Building Character Voice

Now that we have a stronger sense of the mechanics of dialogue and what we don't need to include, let's take a closer look at how to build unique and specific voices.

Everything a character says comes from a collection of knowledge and experiences combined with psychological makeup. Experiences that impact word choices and dialogue include things like education, geographic region, parental language use, work history, intelligence, and how literally a character sees the world.

By applying aspects of a character's backstory to their dialogue, we can create more distinct ways of speaking. Using regionalisms, either for where a story is set or where a specific character is from, can help build a distinct voice. For example, does your character say "pop" or "soda"? At the grocery store, does your character push a cart or a buggy? When eating a meal at night, is it supper or dinner?

It's also useful to identify the character's career, education, and areas of expertise, even if those details aren't included in the story. I spent a few years working in the automotive industry. If a car won't start, I might talk about spark, fuel, and compression. That's much different than someone with no experience who might simply say, "I turn the key, and nothing happens."

We often speak like our parents or other relatives, from grammatical choices like "ain't" to word choices and expressions, such as "tin foil" rather than aluminum foil, or "it pleases me greatly," an expression many of my family members and I use because my granny used to say it.

A character's dialogue may also change based on their age. A three-year-old might say they want "noodles," but an adult will say spaghetti. An older person might say "davenport" while a younger person might say couch or sofa. Pay close attention to stereotypes, however. Not everyone over fifty is computer illiterate, and not everyone under fifty has never heard of the Beatles.

One of the best ways to build stronger dialogue is to pay close attention to how people express themselves in the real world. Consider a romantic partner; how do they change when no one else is around versus at a crowded party? Think about co-workers and employers; how do they speak to each other, and does it change when customers are around? Sometimes we are overly formal in public when we want to hide an intimate relationship.

Dialogue versus Action

Another way to show character is to demonstrate a difference between what characters say and what characters do. Depending on the point of view of the story, we can also show a difference between what characters say and do and *think*. This allows readers to experience the complications of human communication and interactions. Let's use Patricia as an example.

We know Patricia's daughter is missing, and the chief of police is Patricia's ex-boyfriend from high school. She broke his heart when they were teenagers, but now she needs his help. Here is an example of how we might see differences in what she thinks, says, and does.

Patricia sat across the desk from Peter. Though gray showed at his temples, the boyish dimples still appeared on his face when he smiled. A twinge of desire shot through her. "Is there anything else you need from me? I have to go to work."

Peter looked surprised. "I'm sure your boss would give you the day off given the circumstances."

The rent was due. The electric bill was late. She'd let her own health insurance go. "It's better if I keep busy."

Patricia could see other people through the windows in Peter's office, but the soundproofing was good, and the room sat quiet. She knew she needed to stand, but her legs felt weak.

Peter watched her, his expressive brown eyes filled with questions. About Kelly, about her, about them.

He leaned back in his chair. "I'll call you if I hear anything."

Patricia nodded but continued to sit.

In this example, Patricia says she has to get to work rather than bring up what she's really thinking about, which is the relationship between the two of them. This shows readers a difference between what she thinks and what she says. Then she tells Peter that going to work is about how she would rather stay busy, not that her job is hanging on by a thread. She's protecting herself by not admitting how close she is to being fired and the tenuousness of her financial situation. Again, this shows a difference between her thoughts and her words. Next, rather than get up, she continues sitting. This shows a difference between what she says and what she does. Lastly, we can guess at Peter's thoughts: He's wondering how she can go to work with her daughter missing and why her boss wouldn't give her a day off. But he doesn't ask any questions even though we can guess he's curious.

Each one of those differences builds a better picture of the characters and their dynamic. Subtext can activate reader engagement because it's up to the reader to interpret meaning, which is part of the fun of reading.

The Purposes of Dialogue

Now that we have a better understanding of how to build dialogue, create distinct character voices, include exposition, and write contrasting character thoughts, words, and actions, let's take a closer look at the function of dialogue.

One of the most important roles for dialogue is to move the story forward. Dialogue can replace information in prose, but it should not repeat information already in prose. Here's an example:

Patricia picked up the phone to call Kelly. It went directly to voice mail, so she left a message. "Hi, Kelly, it's me. I'm worried that my calls keep going straight to voice mail. Please call me as soon as you get this."

The information in prose (Patricia calls Kelly but it goes straight to voice mail) is then repeated in the dialogue. We can either take out the prose or the dialogue.

Taking out the prose could look like this:

Patricia hit the call button on her cell. "Hi, Kelly, it's me. My calls keep going straight to voice mail. Please call me as soon as you get this."

We know Patricia is calling someone on her cell. The dialogue shows us who she calls and that the call keeps going to voice mail.

Taking out some of the information in the dialogue could look like this:

Patricia called Kelly's cell. It went straight to voice mail. "Please call me."

Here, the prose shows readers that the call goes to voice mail, and the dialogue shows Patricia's anxiety about not being able to reach her daughter.

Another way that dialogue can move the story forward is by providing exposition the reader is not aware of yet. Here's an example of that:

Patricia looked at Peter. "You've gone gray since I last saw you."

Peter ran a hand through his hair. "It has been over fifteen years."

If we haven't previously referenced how long it has been since they last saw each other, this line of dialogue informs readers of new information that moves the story forward and further illustrates the dynamic between them.

Dialogue Shows Character Conflict

Another way to move the story forward with dialogue is to show character conflict, either internal or external. Let's return to Patricia's story for some examples.

Peter leaned forward. His eyes bored into Patricia's. "Is there anything else I should know about your daughter? Drugs? Boyfriend? Girlfriend? Did the two of you have a fight?"

"She does not use drugs, and she only hangs out with a group of friends. She isn't dating anyone."

Peter waited, his face expectant.

"Yes. We had a fight. But it wasn't that big of a deal. It can't have had anything to do with her going missing."

"You should have told me that before."

Here we see some of Patricia's internal conflict. She had a fight with her daughter, but she doesn't want to admit to Peter—or herself—that the fight might be the cause of her daughter's disappearance.

Here's an example of external conflict:

Peter leaned forward. His eyes bored into Patricia's. "Does she have a boyfriend or girlfriend?"

"Teens are all about going out in groups today. They don't pair up like kids did when we were in school."

"Teenagers still fall in love. We didn't have a corner on that market."

Patricia didn't need the reminder. "I would know if she was in love with someone. We don't have any secrets."

"Teens always have secrets. We did."

This dialogue sets up new information and shows conflict between Patricia and Kelly and between Patricia and Peter, moving the story forward in important ways that aren't yet spelled out for the readers. The scene poses questions and compels readers to keep going.

Kelly does have secrets from Patricia, which will be explored and revealed later in the plot. Patricia and Peter had a secret, and now that we have planted the seed, readers want to know what it was and how it relates to the present day. For example, maybe Kelly is Peter's daughter, and the secret was a pregnancy that Peter thought was terminated, but Patricia hid the truth from him. Or maybe Peter and Patricia ran away, planning to get married, but chickened out and returned home. Peter could be referencing that experience from their past to illustrate to Patricia what Kelly could be up to. Regardless, the dialogue moves the story forward.

Dialogue Provides Character Voice

Many factors work together to build a unique character voice: the distinctive way a character speaks, the content of their dialogue, and how the dialogue shows conflict and moves the story forward.

The last aspect of dialogue we should be aware of is our tendency to use filler words, often at the beginning of a sentence. Words such as well, so, and basically rarely help the dialogue, and in fact, can bog it down. Even though we might speak that way in the real world, think of writing dialogue as costing money. If every word has a cost to it, is it worth the money to buy a "so" or a "well"? Take that word out and read the sentence again, and you'll see the improvement.

Let's look at an example from Patricia and Peter.

"So, Peter. What are you going to do next?"

"Well, Patricia, I am going to contact bus stations, taxis, and train stations with photo of Kelly."

Better: "What are you going to do next?"

"Contact bus stations, taxis, and train stations with a photo of Kelly."

Notice I've cut so and well, but I've also cut the unnecessary use of Peter and Patricia's names. We also don't need Peter to say "I am" going to contact bus stations. He's describing his own actions, so a simple response with exactly what he plans is tighter and more natural.

Now that we are armed with an understanding of what dialogue can do and how to best incorporate it into prose, let's do an exercise to assess the dialogue in a current work in progress.

Exercise 8: Improving Dialogue

Strong dialogue can make a manuscript pop for an agent or editor. Making sure dialogue moves the story forward, sounds unique to each character, and shows character conflict can move a manuscript from the slush pile to the yes pile.

Step One: Choose a section of existing material that contains dialogue. For those working on a new project, use material generated from the earlier exercises. Apply the information from this chapter to assess the following.

1. Does the dialogue move the story forward?
2. Does the dialogue show character voice through distinct language?
3. Does the dialogue show character conflict, both internal and external?

Step Two: Using the answers to these questions, rewrite the section to improve each of these aspects. If working on a brand-new project and there isn't any dialogue, either write a new scene or add dialogue to an existing scene. One technique is to pick two characters and get them talking to each other. Choose a room and a topic, and let the characters guide the dialogue. After generating a section of dialogue, return to Step One.

Step Three: Read the new section out loud or have it read to you. Use the Auto Read function in Word (under Review in the header, click on Read Aloud), or ask a friend or two to help you out. Ask yourself these questions:

1. How does the dialogue land on your ear? Does it sound natural?
2. Does it have any filler words (um, well, so, basically)?
3. Does it do all three of the aspects included in Step One?

If it does, great. You have a solid piece of dialogue for that section of material. If it doesn't, rewrite again until the dialogue feels natural, the character voices feel distinct, and the dialogue fulfills the questions above.

Step Four: Moving forward, continue to reference this exercise for any section of dialogue, especially if it feels forced or unnecessary.

| 8 |

Final Thoughts

> Without characters, a story has no plot.
> Without a plot, a story has no point.

Plot is built primarily from characters in action. Plot also relies on thoughts, reflections, and dialogue, all of which stem from character. Without compelling characters, even the most dynamic of plots can still fail.

What characters say, do, think, and feel all combine to create a connection with the reader—one that often remains with a reader long after "the end."

Whether a story is an action-packed thriller, a steamy, hot romance, or a poignant coming-of-age, we remember how characters make us feel. We connect with them because they want something, something stands in the way, and it matters whether they achieve their goals or not. Even in memoir, we engage with the author based on their super-objectives.

When considering the characters in a work in progress, whether rewriting or generating the first draft, keep these four key principles in mind.

- Readers engage with characters they can root for, whether they like them or not.
- Readers connect with characters who want something but something stands in the way.
- Exposition is most effective when limited to what readers need, when they need it.
- The strongest dialogue moves the story forward.

When building characters, even minor ones, consider what their objectives are for each scene, and if a character has a lot of page time, discover their super-objective for the full manuscript.

Goals Define Character

Real people may not be defined by their goals, but fictional characters are. Further, memoirists can be defined by their goals in the specific part of their life they describe in their work. If a character does not have a super-objective pulling them through the story, there's likely nothing to pull the reader through the story.

The success or failure of a character to achieve their super-objective determines the outcome of the manuscript, not whether the manuscript is a success or failure. Whether it's happy, sad, poignant, or bittersweet, the final emotional state of the protagonist—and the reader—comes from the character's relationship with their ultimate goal. A character can achieve their goal, and it's good (happy ending). A character can fail to reach their goal and it's bad (sad ending). A character can fail to achieve their goal but gain something else (bittersweet or poignant ending or happy if it's something great). A character can achieve their goal and realize it wasn't worth it (tragedy). There are lots of ways a book can end, but that big question of whether or not a character succeeds or fails at their quest will be answered.

Final Exercise

This final exercise is broken into two parts, the first for those working on an existing draft, the second for those building a new project through the use of this guidebook.

Existing Manuscript

Work through the full manuscript with an intentional rewrite to strengthen character development. Use this exercise to strengthen all the characters, not just the major ones. This will be a time-consuming and complex exercise if done correctly, so take all the time it needs. It will make the material stronger.

Step One: Print out the first chapter or scene.

Step Two: Read slowly and carefully. For each character that arrives in a scene, even minor characters, ask what their objective is in the scene. Make a note of the objective in the margin. Do the character's actions support that objective? Would another objective make their actions more interesting? Would different actions relate more to their objective? Make notes on the page with ideas for new objectives, different actions, and the subsequent impact on that character's behavior.

Step Three: Depending on personal preference, either rewrite the scene on the hard copy first, before moving it to the computer, or start on the computer and rewrite the scene based on the notes in the margin.

Step Four: Print out the next chapter or scene. Did the rewrite on the previous section change anything for this chapter? If yes, make notes in the margins. If no, repeat steps two and three for this section.

Step Five: Continue in this manner through the entire manuscript. Keep in mind that changes in one scene may not impact the next one but could impact a scene a few chapters later. This exercise will take tremendous focus. Keep the notes for all the scenes available for reference during the process.

Step Six: After completing all the scenes in this manner, let the material sit for a period of time, at least a week, though more is good, too. Then read through the new draft and identify any other character issues. Do this until the characters are as complex and active as possible throughout the entire manuscript.

New Project

Step One: Print out what is most likely the earliest scene currently written. Don't worry if it isn't the opening scene, but it should come before any other scene already written.

Step Two: Read slowly and carefully. For each character that arrives in a scene, even minor characters, determine their objective. Make a note in the margin. Do the character's actions support that objective? Would another objective make their actions more interesting? Would different actions make more sense based on that objective? Make notes on the page with ideas for new objectives or actions and the subsequent impact on that character's behavior.

Step Three: Depending on personal preference, either rewrite the scene on the hard copy before typing it into the computer or start at the computer and rewrite the scene based on the notes in the margin.

Step Four: Print out that scene again and make notes on the hard copy about what led the protagonist into that scene and what their likely actions might be based on what happens next.

Step Five: If there is clearly a missing scene leading into this one, write that scene next.

If the current scene is the opening scene or chapter for the manuscript, take a look at the other scenes already written, and see if any of them would go next. If they do, use the information from **Step Four** and rewrite the next scene. If there isn't a clear next scene, use the information from **Step Four** and write the next scene.

Step Six: Using this process of rewriting a scene, identifying what the protagonist would do next, and either inserting or writing the next scene, progress through the manuscript or back up and write earlier missing scenes. Use all the previous work on character objectives, super-objectives, landscapes, and backstory to flesh out the characters and move them toward their ultimate goals.

Continue with this until you have a complete draft. This might take a month, or this might take a year or longer. There is no deadline for completing a first draft.

Step Seven: Once there is a completed first draft, go back through the exercises in this book, and apply the exercises for a work in progress.

Congratulations on reaching the end of this guide!

So much goes into writing a manuscript of any length. Whether a short story, novel, script, or memoir, just completing a first draft is a worthy accomplishment. Ready to keep working? Use the other books in this series to strengthen the plot and work on rewrites. It may also be time to bring in a professional outside eye. Feel free to reach out to me or any of the other editors at Allegory Editing. From developmental editing to copy editing and proofreading, it has become more and more important for writers to utilize all the opportunities available and produce the most polished manuscript possible before beginning to query or starting the publishing process. Find us on the web at www.allegoryediting.com

ABOUT THE AUTHOR

Mark Perlstein

Elena Hartwell has spent years supporting writers and constructing stories. Her award-winning and bestselling works include the Eddie Shoes mysteries and *All We Buried* (written under Elena Taylor). Her plays have been seen around the US and UK, garnering critical acclaim and stellar reviews. As a developmental editor she has worked with hundreds of writers, most recently as senior editor and director of programming for the boutique editing house, Allegory Editing. She regularly teaches writing workshops and enjoys helping others achieve their writing dreams.

To learn more visit www.elenahartwell.com

ACKNOWLEDGMENTS

Thrilled this little book has finally seen the light of day. The last few years have been hard on all of us, so I hope this guide will help motivate your writing and give you insights into telling your best story.

There are so many people I'm grateful for, without whom I would never have crossed the finish line.

To Amy Cecil Holm, who went above and beyond copy editor and proofreader. I'm more than happy to steal all your great ideas. To Andrea Karin Nelson and Christine Pinto, for always making me a better writer. To Malissa Winicki who always finds time to answer my questions and be my expert in many things. To Courtenay Schurman 5H, we got this together! To Sheila Sobel, who remains my anchor in a challenging world. And last but not least, to my darling hubby, JD Hammerly, I'm so glad we found our Paradise.